W9-AXG-174

# STAGE DECORATION

*Design by* Gordon Craig *for a stage setting:*
*"A Palace, a Slum and a Stairway."* 1907.

# STAGE DECORATION

BY SHELDON CHENEY

TWO HUNDRED FIFTY-SIX
ILLUSTRATIONS

THE JOHN DAY COMPANY
NEW YORK : MCMXXVIII

FIRST PUBLISHED, JANUARY, 1928
SECOND PRINTING, JULY, 1928



PRINTED IN THE U.S.A.
FOR THE JOHN DAY COMPANY, INC.
BY E. L. HILDRETH & CO., BRATTLEBORO, VT.

## ABOUT THE AUTHOR

SHELDON CHENEY was born in Berkeley, California, in 1886. After his graduation from the University of California in 1908, he devoted himself for a time to writing magazine articles on the theatre and arts. In 1916 he founded the *Theatre Arts Magazine*, and was its editor for three years. From 1920 to 1926 he was actively engaged in theatre production work with the Actors' Theatre and other producing organizations in New York. For the past year he has been traveling in Europe, studying foreign theatre methods, and he is now continuing his research and investigations abroad.

In addition to *Stage Decoration*, Mr. Cheney has written the following books: *The New Movement in the Theatre* (1916); *The Art Theatre* (1917); and *A Primer of Modern Art* (1923).

# CONTENTS

# LIST OF ILLUSTRATIONS

*With sources and acknowledgements.*

PLATES OF MODERN STAGE DECORATION

NOTE: *In most cases where sources of the modern plates have not been indicated and acknowledgments not printed, the reproductions are made by courtesy of* Theatre Arts Monthly, *a magazine that has been made a repository for the best material pertinent to the modern theatre, in stagecraft as in other fields. In a few cases reproductions are from photographs and designs in the author's collection.*

# PREFACE

*MY object is to write (or arrange) a book about stage forms and stage settings which will afford the reader a bird's-eye view of this element of theatre art throughout the ages, with a somewhat closer view of the revolutionary changes in thought upon the subject, and in practice, during the last thirty years.*

*I am therefore setting out to treat stage decoration in two ways: first in a very brief résumé of its chronological development, from the beginnings of Western drama in Athens to the perfected nineteenth-century picture-frame theatre, and then more thoroughly through twentieth-century accomplishment in the field of a simplified realism, and forward to the most recent essays toward a space stage or a formal architectural stage; and into this record I plan to imbed an estimate of visual decorativeness as an integral and contributive part of theatre art.*

*My definition of stage decoration is broad enough to include not only what we used to call "the scenery," but the entire physical aspect of the stage-half of the theatre building, with whatever may have been set up there by way of ornamentation or background, if any, and as lighted and peopled by actors—and I try to think always of this complete physical "stage form" in relation to an audience seated in the auditorium half of the building.*

*Up to this time no one has attempted to write a book on the subject in so comprehensive a way. In gathering the material I have become sensible that what is really needed is a three-volume work: the first volume to cover the history of stage forms and setting from the beginnings through the era of the painted perspective scene in the proscenium-frame theatre; the second volume to treat of contempo-*

*rary stage decoration as it is being practiced on nine-tenths of our "better" stages, in a modified realistic picture setting, tastefully simplified, plastically conceived, and prettily composed; and the third volume treating "modernism" on the stage, in the narrower sense, as a parallel to modernist painting, sculpture, architecture and religion, as a revolution against the realistic representation and the pictured setting, and including the Expressionist experiments, the formal stages, the space stages and theatric "constructions."*

*As it is, I have modified my original plan for this smaller volume, which was to have been entitled "Modern Stage Decoration," to make it include the short historical résumé as a part of the introductory essay, and also a series of forty historical plates—because such background material has nowhere been made available. (I frankly include this summary as a merely tentative contribution to a subject surprisingly neglected by students and artists.) And at the other end of my show of contemporary general practice, I have added examples of experiment along all the lines of radicalism; because I believe that the 250-year reign of realism and pictorialism is about over, and that the key to the theatre of to-morrow is in the hands of the radicals. Thus my book, which would roughly approximate volume two if the threatened trilogy came into being, is now extended at both ends, to look backward and forward—and therefore goes forth to parade as a* general *work on stage decoration.*

*In writing of decoration, by the way, I am not treating or leading up to a new art of the theatre in which background is glorified. To guard against the zeal of those who scent in any attempt to emphasize scene a danger to the dramatic and acting values, let me say that I see decoration as a contributive craft, second to the play, to the actor, to direction. Important as it is (and the ensemble or synthesis of stage arts is incomplete and corrupt without it), there is value in it only as the designer sees clearly the importance of these other elements. But while I distrust isolation of any fragmentary art or craft, I feel that a serious study of stage decoration in relation to the whole art of the theatre can only broaden and aid the artist in whatever department of the theatre he may be, actor, playwright or regisseur.*

*I shall try to make the book as practical as possible, without any intention of going into matters of construction and machinery, by including among the illustrations photographs rather than drawings, in those cases where adequate photographs are available. In some examples, however, I have found the artist's sketch a truer indication of the actual aspect achieved, and in a few others I have seen typically theatric possibilities in a drawing and include it for illustration of a particular point. In the matter of photographs, I am specially grateful to Francis Bruguiere, whose pictures of productions in New York I am using to the number of twenty.*

*To the editors of* Theatre Arts Monthly *I am extraordinarily indebted, because nearly one-third of the illustrations in this book are being printed from plates owned by that publication. I may add that ten years ago when I was editor of* Theatre Arts, *the plan of the book first took shape, and the magazine then began publishing examples not only of the best current staging but of outstanding productions in the past history of the progressive movement, with an eye to the possible collecting of the plates later. Edith J. R. Isaacs, under whose editorship and personal direction the magazine has so extended its usefulness, has been not only a sympathetic advisor in this tardy gathering of the material but a friend and helper at a hundred difficult turns. But for her, publication would have been longer delayed and the material far less complete.*

*The book belongs creatively, of course, to those artists whose work is illustrated, far more than to me, a critic and collector. To Gordon*

*Craig I owe exceptional gratitude. The American designers are in so many cases close personal friends that I cannot say just where professional obligation leaves off and friendship begins—so I choose no individual ones, but record a general "Thank you!" for unvarying and cordial coöperation. To the many artists in Europe who have supplied photographs, I am likewise thankful, and to those several authors and publishers who have permitted reproduction of plates from their books, a courtesy noted with individual acknowledgments in the list of plates and sources that immediately precedes this preface. Louis Jouvet and Andrew Stephenson have made special drawings for the volume, a service for which the reader will join me in being grateful. I am indebted to John Mason Brown and to Donald Oenslager for reading the text in proof, and for suggestions and corrections.*

SHELDON CHENEY

*October, 1927*
*Scarborough, New York*

# PART I

## STAGE DECORATION

## I

## DEFINITION AND THEORY

STAGE decoration is, in simplest terms, the craft of creating an adequate and appropriate background for theatric action.

This definition is worded broadly, to signify either the designing and placing in the theatre of special "settings," their lighting and their coördination with the other visual elements of production, or the building of a formal stage to be used as the scene of the action through many productions without change or adornment. Such a definition takes into consideration the revolution in thought upon the subject during the last thirty years, a comparatively brief period during which the change was greater than for 250 years previous; for at any time during the eighteenth and nineteenth centuries one would have been told without thought or hesitation that stage decoration was the art of *painting scenery* for the theatre.

There are so many kinds of theatre, so many legitimate forms of theatric and dramatic presentation and representation, that a definition must be elastic and elemental if it is not to prove unduly exclusive. The one that stressed painting was right for its own era, which happened to be a long one, but it excluded most of what had been accomplished in stage setting in the Greek theatre, the Roman theatre, the mediaeval theatre and the Elizabethan theatre. The greatest two world flowerings of dramatic art occurred on stages where, so far as we can learn, the painted setting was almost unknown. The picture mode in stage decoration, indeed, has been extant only during one-tenth of the history of the theatre in time, and only during an era that has been comparatively lacking in those high qualities that characterized the plays of Shakespeare, Aeschylus, Sophocles and Euripides.

But there are still other characteristics of decoration as practiced in the eighteenth and nineteenth centuries that make the definitions then current inaccurate and unsafe for application to-day. Two standard statements were worded thus: "Stage decoration is the art of making striking stage pictures," and "The scene should be considered a splendor added to the representation of a play." Here is expressed or implied what we of the twentieth century consider a fundamental fault of staging in the painted-perspective era: the making of scenery was considered as a separate and independent rather than a contributive art, was seldom coördinated with the arts of the playwright, the actor and the costumer, and was glorified at the expense of the play and acting, with, in brief, "a splendor added." We know now that any sort of splendor in the decoration—if it is not too dangerous for us to compass at all—must grow out of a vision of all the elements of production, coördinated and integrated, else it will be destructive of true theatric emotion.

If one is seeking something else in the theatre than the theatre's own essential gifts—seeking a picture, say—then one may grant the nineteenth-century definitions full validity. As a matter of fact, decoration was so pursued on its own account at one time, staging was so over-stressed, that the leading French playhouse, home of the *Comédie Française* and then of the Paris *Opéra*, lost its name of "theatre" entirely and was called the "*Salle des Machines*." During this period the making of scenes and "effects" resulted from a perfect marvel of ingenuity, and people came to the theatre to enjoy compelling pictures, clever transformations and eye-deceiving "stunts." To the extent that these added attractions were successful, in that measure the true acted art of the theatre suffered eclipse. Even so recently as 1913 Van Dyke Browne wrote* that "the ancient Greeks and Romans were very fond of the drama and have left us some great plays . . . but they did not realize the value of scenery." The self-satisfaction implied in that statement, its frank claim for the added values, grates on the ears as we read it to-day.

There was a time when the twentieth-century revolutionaries went to the very opposite extreme, crying out for the suppression of decoration in any dynamic sense of the word. Even the term "decorator" came to be regarded with suspicion, if not hostility. During this pendulum swing away from display setting, the idea gained currency that the stage form and stage setting must never be considered as more than *mere* background. Maxime

* Van Dyke Browne: *Secrets of Scene Painting and Stage Effects*. London. [1913.]

Dethomas once wrote that the *décor* should above all else be a good servant of the play. Georg Fuchs, with the anti-display thought in mind, added wisely that the best servants are those who speak the least. But Jacques Rouché summed up the matter, with a reservation, as follows: "*Le décor est le bon serviteur du drame; il ne doit parler qu'en cas de nécessité.*"

Adolphe Appia, one of the two outstanding prophets and pioneers of the new movement, went even farther, practically advocating the total abolishment of setting. He wrote that "everything inanimate" should be removed from the scene, that the actor after all was the only essential element in the *mise-en-scène*, and that the object of stage setting should be to disembarrass him of distracting surroundings. It is due very largely to this theory and to the stimulus of Appia's writings that light, a living rather than an inanimate medium, has come to take so important a place in contemporary staging.

But even if in exceptional cases an isolated pool of light can be achieved for the action—and this type of setting will find full treatment near the end of the present essay—it is possible only for limited numbers of actors and a very limited range of movement; and for the purposes of a working theory it is safe to assume that sooner or later something comes into view by way of permanent stage platform and walls, or drops or screens behind and around the action.

This might indeed be the starting point for any treatise on stage decoration in its physical aspect: everything that exists has surroundings. Nothing can be revealed, nothing can appear or move before an audience, without background or surroundings. And one may well question whether there is such a thing as "mere" background in an absolute sense, an unnoticeable *milieu*.

It is natural, moreover, to make surroundings pleasant, and who can draw a line of demarkation between that instinct and the urge to decorate? We may take it almost as axiomatic that, whether consciously designed for effect or not, the background will, by the nature, quality or appeal of its shape, color, material, evoke some particular sort of emotion.

If the background, then, is not to be neutral only, not merely a "filler," the next question is: *how far* should it go dynamically, constructively, toward localizing the action, toward creating mood, toward reënforcing the emotion projected by the play and actors? Those artists who are only a shade more positive than the suppressionists, believe that for our over-localized contemporary drama it should, without being too literal, *suggest* the place or the nature of the place chosen by the dramatist. Beyond that there is the far more important requisite of creating atmosphere, of slyly putting the audience into the spirit of the action, of intensifying quietly the intended emotion. This intensification, this reënforcement, through the power of line, proportion and color, may be considered, if you wish, as a parallel to off-stage music, to an accompaniment of sound, in its emotional effectiveness. It helps to attune the audience to the proper mood for drama.

The next shade of opinion is that decoration may properly become not only a reënforcement of the author's intention but a completion of his thought, a truly creative and dynamic contribution. Without fearing that we are in danger of getting back to nineteenth-century separation of functions, or to over-development of settings, we may even accept Lee Simonson's definition of "scenic art, which is the creation of plastic forms and spaces that are an integral part of the acting of any play and project its meaning."* Incidentally it was this same artist who had written eight years earlier that "the importance of scenery is the importance of a background." The difference between these two definitions measures pretty accurately the advance in thought on the part of a large group of designers during the decade from 1915 to 1925. When they were in the first flush of revolt they had gone to the extreme of demanding just as little setting as possible—so that that became the period of curtains, screens and colorless walls; whereas now they have assumed again a more definitely creative duty, an interpretative function. It is an unusual theorist these days who does not grant the decorator a constructive part in heightening mood and intensifying emotion.

It was Lee Simonson again who wrote that the business of the designer is "the search for forms which have interpretative significance and the devising, in relation to the shape of the modern theatres, of spaces that are dramatically expressive." This implies a further step from mere back-

* *Theatre Arts Monthly*, June, 1924.

ground toward dynamic modernism, paralleling the tendency in painting, sculpture and architecture toward a greater reliance on that vague but enormously important thing called "form." I have no intention here of plunging deep into the theories of modernist art. But it is well to point out that the progression from the romantic excursions and then the naturalistic studies of the nineteenth century, in the graphic arts, to a pretty Impressionism, then a simplified decorativeness, and finally into the several channels of anti-realism and Expressionism, has a chronological parallel in staging. In the contemporary theatre the suppression of realism, the grasping at abstraction, the return to an emphasis on the stage as stage (as against the realist's careful disguise of the stage as such), the utilization of linear and spatial relationships rather than depicted background, intensification of emotion by every means belonging to the physical theatre even to the point of distortion of the outward aspects of life—all this is a narrowing in to Expressionism, to an intensified emotional expressiveness through the formal qualities of the theatre.

Back in the days of the glorification of scene painting as a separate art, there was a theory that a stage setting must "hit the eye" the instant the curtain was raised, and its degree of success or failure was rated on whether it "got a hand" or not. Audiences became trained to watch for opportunities to approve thus audibly the work of the painter or to condemn by silence, whether the scene was the garden of *Twelfth Night*, or *Valhalla* or the famous cabbage patch of Mrs. Wiggs. The whole proceeding, of course, was destructive of dramatic unity, and was predicated on the idea that the "artist" might seek approbation on his own account rather than as a contributor to a successful total impression. It is necessary to keep clear the distinction between this sort of parading of the settings and the utilization of the physical aspect of the stage to strike the keynote to emotion. For the decorators, the very ones who protested the over-stressing of decoration, have returned to the idea that the setting has an immediate initial duty, not of "knocking 'em cold," but of quietly letting the audience into the secret of the drama's locale and mood, and perhaps reminding them that this is the theatre and not life. Robert Edmond Jones, long known as an artist who was most content when his settings fitted the production so perfectly that they were not noticed, has given expression to a theory, strictly in line with Expressionism, that the scene when the curtain rises should lead the spectator to say to himself, "It is evident that this play we are about to see is no common play. It is evident that these men and women who will appear before us are no common mummers. These are Actors, Seers, Sayers. Let us honor them. For by their inspiration they intimate immortality."* Raymond Jonson had something of the same conception when he noted that "the art of stage decoration aims at setting the point of entrance into the new world." André Boll† has given expression to the ingenious idea that the setting should be just assertive or dynamic enough so that it will place the play and noticeably create atmosphere during *the first few minutes* of an act, and thereafter recede into the flow of the play to the extent of losing all appeal on its own account.

The English term "stage decoration" is generally understood as covering far more than is implied in the French word *décor,* including costume design, lighting and a general visual rhythm. The French *mise-en-scène,* on the other hand, includes the whole design of the actors' movements, everything that goes to the placing of the play on the stage. Indeed, de Fouquières‡ divided the art of the theatre into two parts, the dramatic art, including all that is properly the work or province of the poet, and the *mise-en-scène,* which is the combined or common work of all those who to any extent collaborate in the representation. The emphasis on the complete work of placing the play in the scene suggests the breadth of the German term *regie,* the province of that comparatively new figure, the master of the theatre, the *regisseur.*

No student of the modern stage, I think, can understand the spirit of contemporary staging, can realize the sincerity of the designers in their willingness to make their contribution subserviently, until he understands with what energy, even passion, the recent revolutionaries have called for this regisseur, for an all-powerful, all-seeing master of staging, the artist-director supreme. He is the new, the typically twentieth-century artist in the theatre, and his function is the harmonizing of all the elements of

* From the Foreword to *Drawings for the Theatre,* by Robert Edmond Jones. New York, 1925.

† André Boll: *Du Décor de Théâtre.* Paris [1925].

‡ L. Becq de Fouquières: *l'Art de la Mise en Scène.* Paris, 1884.

the complex work of production—not only harmonizing, but of imagining and assembling them. In Germany, too, there is the less broad word *inscenierung*, but it is not borrowed into our language as these others occasionally are. We are likely to say that our "stage decorators" (itself an inexact term) design their settings in accordance with a "regisseur's" vision of a "mise-en-scène"—a process no more international and mixed in wording than are the sources from which the designer has developed his new theory of staging.

While thus running through, by way of introduction, various definitions and interpretations of "stage decoration"—without, I hope, encroaching too far on the story of the actual changes in method during the last quarter-century, as that story will be told in later pages—I have purposely avoided going into the matter of changing definitions of the total art of the theatre, into the corresponding revolutionary shifting of theatrical theory as a whole. This much should be said, however: in the consideration of the theatre there was for a very great era an unfortunate incompleteness of vision, so that the writing of plays, the literary aspect of drama, was thought of as the sum of theatre art, and the whole subject was treated in learned circles as a department of literature; and again in a different time, the art of acting was taken to be the summation of stage art, "the age of great actors." During those periods the art of stage decoration was being pursued in a separatist fashion. But the complete view of the theatre, the belief that the several contributive arts are all of a necessary importance, the feeling that a theatrical unity must underlie the play, the acting, the visual elements, the *regie*—these are ideas rediscovered during the last thirty years and now stressed as never before. If you will read through the important theories of the theatre down the ages, you will find that there is seldom mention of this larger unity (although unity is stressed always as an element of playwriting), and little mention of coördination except in acting. The conception of a synthetic art—not in the scientific sense in which we speak of synthetic gold, or synthetic food or synthetic gin, but as a perfectly fused, completely-seen group-art—is a thing of contemporary thought. Or if you prefer *rhythm* to synthesis, let us say that the moderns insist, as never before, that an all-pervading rhythm inform every element of the production on the stage.

So any working definition of the art of the theatre to-day has to emphasize the presentation of a play by actors on a stage, through a flow of action, *with that fusion of all the contributive stage arts which makes the drama live for its audience at its highest possible emotional intensity*. Within this larger definition there should be special emphasis on *action* as the essentially theatric core of the art; but either action in the sense of movement (as in early ritual drama and in the recently highly developed dance-dramas), or in the sense of the unfolding of a story or drama by actors using speech largely for expressiveness.

If the artists of the last quarter-century have thus widened the definition of theatre art, and have changed profoundly both the theory and practice of stage decoration, they have also outgrown one of their own early misconceptions. They now know better than to believe that reform in stage-craft alone will result in a new and typically modern art of the theatre. A decade ago, I think, many of us fancied that with decoration taking its place in a synthesized art of the theatre, a new and glorious form of stage production had been born. Having gained a further perspective on the situation, we now recognize that true new forms of theatre art are not hatched so easily, that a coördinate revolution in playwriting and acting is necessary before a complete new art is likely to emerge.

And yet, looking back, we know that an altogether extraordinary gain has been made. We know that the designers of settings have joined with the playwrights, the directors and some of the more enlightened actors in an attitude that accepts the whole effect from the stage as the important thing, not the play alone or the acting or the scenic values. We know that stage-craft during thirty years has made a steady march toward the typically *theatrical*, after centuries of practice in imitation of easel-painting and photography. We know that current staging is at least simple, unpretentious, aiming to dress the drama, new or old, appropriately and harmoniously. We see the way cleared for the emergence of a typically modern theatre art, and we have seen thrusts toward it. And in all this gain, the men who have been concerned with stage decoration, the men who originally set out to change only the scene or the form of the theatre, have been leaders. They have destroyed both the physical and the theoretical barriers to a new art.

## II

## THE HISTORICAL BACKGROUND

THE record of the changing stage, and of stage decoration in the larger sense, spans twenty-four centuries. There were probably important developments of dramatic ritual, if not of drama and theatre, in the earlier periods of which mankind has scant or no knowledge. But for the Western world as known, the theatre was born in Athens. As Greek life disentangled itself from the veiling background, other arts emerged before this one of dramatic action. One of its roots, indeed, goes back to recited literature; but the main source of *acted* drama was in religious ritual. The new art sprang out of one element of the carnivals and festivals so beloved by the Mediterranean, vine growing peoples, an element combining worship and pleasure, the Dionysian parades and dances.

At first the "theatre" was probably no more than a cleared and marked-out dancing-circle ("orchestra," from the Greek word meaning "to dance"), with spectators standing around; then a hillside hollow with the dancing-circle at its foot. In the circle's center was an altar to Dionysus, and a sacrificial table which a legend tells us became the first "stage"—perhaps only *before* the spectators found the vantage ground of the hillside. At any rate, as the one "actor" separated himself from the dancers, there was added a tent or hut, the "*skene*," in which he could change costume, somewhere beyond the orchestra; and farther back in the area consecrated to Dionysus (if we are still considering Athens, where the first and most important ancient theatre developed) was the temple which some authorities believe helped to give form to the ultimate stage-building.

Here, then, even before there was any constructed building, were the three elements that were to characterize every theatre for centuries to follow: auditorium, orchestra and "skene." These elements have persisted even to the theatres of to-day, but with this difference: the hut, as "scene," ultimately drew into itself the entire acting space, whereas in Greek times the playing was all in the orchestra-circle. So important was the dancing-circle as playing space, indeed, that when the auditorium took truly architectural form it was in the shape of a U, a semi-circle with the ends prolonged, because spectators were content if they looked down on the circle, as there was no stage which the seats must face.

The first mentioned theatres had temporary wooden seats, like the present-day athletic-field bleachers. We may put up our first chronological signpost here, as roughly 500 B.C., because it is recorded that in 499 B.C. the wooden benches built for spectators collapsed, and that a "theatre" was therefore erected—which may have been the first stone theatre. What changes were made in the playing area at this time is unknown, and a controversy of prodigious proportions has raged among scholars for forty years past regarding the form of the stage building during the ensuing fifth and fourth centuries B.C. It now seems established that there was no platform stage in this period, the widely published reconstructions with this feature being erroneously based on knowledge of the later Greek-Roman theatres.

Certainly in the fourth-century theatre at Athens the full dancing-circle was backed by a scene-building considerably longer than the diameter of the circle, with two wings (*paraskenia*) projecting forward, as evidenced by foundations existing to-day. Authorities seem to be fast reaching agreement, too, that a construction more like a colonnade than a platform-stage, called a *proskenion*, was temporarily built between the projecting wings, the whole thus forming a one-story columned structure against the main two-story scene-building behind. The drawing by Professor James Turney Allen, which I am reproducing in plate 2, though frankly conjectural in part, is an essay at reconstructing the earlier fifth-century scene-building, of which no traces remain, on the evidence of the dramas and of certain deductions from relationship of existing orchestra foundations to the known fourth-century arrangement. The drawing approaches as close as we can arrive at this time to an approximation of the scene as it existed in the time of Aeschylus, Sophocles and Euripides: the audience looked down on a dancing-circle, and beyond to a fairly low, dignified, temple-like building. Other scholars have made radically differing conjectural drawings of both the fifth- and fourth-century theatres, and I am reproducing those made by August Frickenhaus to illustrate his theory of the appearance of the Athens theatre in the Lycurgean period, both for their general suggestiveness and because they show the relationship of auditorium and playing area.

As for stage decoration in the stricter sense, the reader should dismiss from his mind the conception of a picture setting for each play, or a specially prepared architectural scene. The stage in this period, as in many others down to Shakespeare's time, was a neutral place, frankly a theatre, and changes of scene were accomplished in the words of the poet.* Scholars of the nineteenth century, unable to think of setting in any other terms than realistic painted backgrounds, made many attempts to discover methods of changing painted settings on the Greek stage of the greatest period, and there are strange drawings of huge painted screens set incongruously on the architectural stage. But there is absolutely no contemporary evidence on the point, and no more argument than the supposition of minds trained to link painting and spectacle with the dramatic art that people as smart as the ancient Greeks must have utilized realistic or spectacular settings. The sole contemporary reference is that of Aristotle to the effect that Sophocles introduced "scenography" for the first time, a statement that may be interpreted as meaning anything from the introduction of a mere indication of place to the presentation of a spectacular interlude. We know that certain machines and effects were invented early; and somewhere along the way a device for summarily *indicating* changes of setting was invented. The *periacti*, or revolving prisms, supposed to have been painted with different scenes in miniature on the three sides, were stood in the acting space, to be turned when desired as indications of change of locale. The descriptions of the mechanism are limited to Roman writers of several centuries later, so that it would be hazardous to attribute habitual use of the device or anything similar to the theatres of the Aeschylean-Sophoclean period. There is also later evidence, none too definite, of a movable platform or a revolving platform on a pivot, called the *eccyclema*, which some scholars believe was

* I originally wrote, "in the words of the poet *and in the imagination of the spectator*." But the spectator does not imagine actual scenes: he has accepted the convention of the theatre—this is art, not life—and his literal mind is stilled. Subconsciously he is open to impressions of pleasing or unpleasing background, of fitting or incongruous surroundings, but he does not stop to picture mentally the missing "place."

widely utilized on the Greek stage, particularly to reveal an interior scene (the generally accepted architectural *proskenion* being considered adequate for the predominating exterior scenes before palaces, temples and houses).

For a brief view of the subject like this, however, it is sufficient to summarize the whole controversial matter by saying that in general the Greek theatre was a distinctly three-part affair—orchestra, auditorium, scene-building—and that the scene-building provided in its pleasing and dignified architectural form practically all the "stage decoration" considered necessary by the dramatists and actors of the time.

In later Greek times, as the scene-building developed, perhaps elsewhere than in Athens, it assumed the form of a high stage (probably the roof of the old *proskenion*) backed by a higher architectural structure. Thus in addition to the acting space in the orchestra there was a platform stage before a permanently decorative architectural wall.

In Roman times the progression continued, until finally all action had been transferred to the platform stage, the old orchestra-circle being cut to a semi-circle and added to the audience space. The auditorium was pushed up against the stage so that it made one architectural unit with the scene-building. The whole affair became massive and ornamental. Where the stage-building of the Greeks had never been more than two stories high (one story above the level that became the later acting platform), the background of the Roman stage was ornamented with intricate architectural relief towering two and even three stories above the raised stage, with an ornamented stage roof above that. The stage floor in existing examples is from three to five feet above the orchestra. The heavily decorated wall that now closed in the acting area on three sides, usually had three doorways in the back and one in each of the projecting side walls. By a convention, which probably had arisen in the transitional Greek-Roman period, the central doorway was understood by the audience to be that of a palace, and the others in the rear wall those of guest chambers; and in regard to the portals at the ends of the stage, a figure entering through that at the right was understood to be from the immediate neighborhood, while one entering at left was understood to be a traveler from a distance.

As to the form of the Roman stage, there can be little controversy, since the ruins now existing, most notably at Orange, Pompeii and Aspendus, afford the basis for exact reconstruction. There is, too, little doubt that the stage wall, while almost too decorative in its own architectural way, served as a permanent, neutral background for most plays of serious import, probably with the suggestive aid of some such device as the revolving *periacti*.

Aside from the regular drama, however, the Romans became lovers of spectacle, and developed a marvelous array of machinery for novel effects; and it may be that in the decadent days they made essays into the field of scene-painting as that art was to develop many centuries later. In view of the contemporary evidence of architectural stages and much machinery, and the significant absence of specific description of scene painting, one may feel fairly sure that Roman decoration and spectacle remained almost wholly in the sphere of the architect and the engineer. Horace threw scathing protests at the populace for its love of the trivial and meretricious "show" elements in the theatre; but nowhere is there reference to any individual painted setting.

Vitruvius, who gives in his work, *Ten Books on Architecture,* instructions for designing Greek and Roman theatres, describes the presumably contemporary (Augustan) stage and *periacti,* as follows:* "The *scaena* itself displays the following scheme. In the center are double doors decorated like those of a royal palace. At the right and left are the doors of the guest chambers. Beyond are spaces provided for decoration—places that the Greeks call περιακτοι because in these places are triangular pieces of machinery which revolve, each having three decorated faces. When the play is to be changed, or when gods enter to the accompaniment of sudden claps of thunder, these may be revolved and present a face differently decorated. Beyond these places are the projecting wings which afford entrances to the stage, one from the forum, the other from abroad.

"There are three kinds of scenes, one called the tragic, another, the comic, and a third, the satyric. Their decorations are different and unlike each other in scheme. Tragic scenes are delineated with columns, pediments, statues, and other objects suited to kings; comic scenes exhibit private dwell-

* Translation of Morris Hicky Morgan, published by the Harvard University Press.

ings, with balconies and views representing rows of windows, after the manner of ordinary dwellings; satyric scenes are decorated with trees, caverns, mountains, and other rustic objects delineated in landscape style."

Efforts have been made to apply the second paragraph to the complete stage scene, arguing from it the existence of full painted settings; but the more reasonable opinion is that this constitutes a description of the "differently decorated" three faces of the *periacti*. Of the machines for "effects" Vitruvius wrote clearly, so that these can be attributed safely to his own time; and there is authoritative evidence that certain Roman theatres had front curtains which were raised from and lowered into a slot along the front of the stage. Again, in summary, only by conjecture or by torturing of the evidence can the stage of the Roman theatre be thought characterized by illusional scene, be considered as anything other than mainly neutral architectural background.

As the classical drama all but disappeared in the darkness that settled over Europe in the early Christian centuries, the buildings that housed it fell into decay; but doubtless acting and drama in more or less fly-by-night forms existed continuously until the next flowerings, in the churches and then as part of the general revival of art and learning that marked the Italian Renaissance. Avoiding futile speculation on the possible forms of stage decoration in the dark centuries, and putting aside for the moment the mediaeval religious drama, I wish to vault over to the theatres that were built in the revived classic tradition in sixteenth-century Italy, because they are the link between the Greek and Roman buildings and our stages of to-day. When the various independent cities and courts that then made up the present Italy were swept by the wave of revived interest in ancient culture, academies were formed to study the arts of the Romans, and with many of these learned societies a prime object was the presentation of classic plays. It was for such a society, the Olympic Academy at Vicenza, founded in 1555, that the famous architect Palladio built the still existing theatre that is sometimes known as the Palladian Theatre and sometimes as the Olympic Theatre of Vicenza. As originally opened in 1584, it was in effect a small Roman theatre roofed over. The auditorium was made more shallow than the typical Roman half-circle, but the general plan and the permanent stage decoration were as exact revivals as the architect's knowledge of the ancient theatres, gained through Vitruvius' works and through examination of ruins, would permit. The architectural ornamentation of the permanent stage wall, although characterized by typical Renaissance modifications, by a general lightening, is clearly copied from the ancient examples, and the five doorways are in the orthodox position. This link between the theatres of Rome and those of to-day is, indeed, more fitted by its design to be called the last of the ancient theatres than it is to be termed the first modern playhouse.

In an addition made after Palladio's death, however, in 1585, is to be found the first imitational scenery known to have been used in a theatre existing to-day. In that year the architect Scamozzi built in behind the five doorways perspective "vistas," relief constructions running back in diminishing size beyond each of the openings in the permanent stage wall. These were not added to increase the acting space, as the portals were not widened, or in answer to any supposed need of the drama for illusive background, but purely for ornament and novelty. They probably were inspired from mixed sources: from a misreading of Vitruvius,* from the vogue for perspectives which had swept the field of the graphic arts, and from the perspective scenes already being used in masques and non-classical dramatic production at the courts. In spite of the fact that the Vicenza stage remained primarily a formal unchanging architectural background for drama, the effect of these "vistas" on stage decoration in other parts of Europe was enormous.

Scamozzi in 1588 built a theatre at Sabbioneta, of which unfortunately the scene no longer exists, with a stage combining the playing space as at Vicenza with an additional ramped stage at the back, in a single diminishing wide perspective scene; and there are plans preserved at Oxford showing that the English architect Inigo Jones, after his trip to Italy in the heart of Shakespearean times, 1613-14, made designs for a theatre with a stage wall more than reminiscent of the Palladian Theatre, a wall which he

* Daniello Barbaro, friend of Palladio, had published in 1556 an edition of Vitruvius in which he showed plans and drawings suggesting that the *periacti* with their painted scenes had been placed in the three doorways of the rear wall of the Roman stage.

pierced with a single large opening, with playing space behind in a perspective scene. Thus one may say that in a sense our modern stage arrived by the gradual widening of the central portal of a revived Roman stage, that the proscenium frame is the enlarged palace doorway of the old permanent stage wall, with the platform for acting pushed through and finally curtained.

As yet the perspective vistas had remained neutral architectural accretions not related to the theory of placing a play realistically. They were imitational, but not representative of a chosen spot out of nature. But the next theatre joins the classic current with that which meantime had been developing out of popular and court dramatic forms. The Farnese Theatre at Parma, usually termed the oldest "modern" playhouse, built in 1618 or 1619, shows the final development of the Roman stage wall into decoration surrounding one large opening, a typical proscenium frame, with the stage gone behind a curtain and presumably demanding a new "setting" for every play. The stage itself and its backing are no longer the scene, the decoration. The auditorium at Parma is designed like half an amphitheatre, and the orchestra floor is available as additional playing space; but the stage is the first of a new type none the less. The mixed form of the auditorium is indication of its derivation out of the court ballroom theatres, while the stage combines elements picked up from the double classic and festival currents.

What went into this newly derived permanent proscenium frame—as significant a feature as any in the whole history of stage building—has to do with both the further development of the perspectives and with the story of painted-picture settings; but now, having established the progression *architecturally* from classic to modern stage form, I must go back and record certain more isolated but intrinsically important phases of stage decoration. Just here, however, I wish to mention that sunlight has now definitely gone out of production in the theatres of Europe. With the roofing over of the building, artificial lighting came in, permanently.

If it was Christianity that jealously killed the drama as Roman civilization gave way to near-darkness, it was in the Christian churches that drama was reborn eight or ten centuries later and long before the lay revival of learning. In the mediaeval church the ritual became dramatized in part, and "Miracle" plays were acted as part of the service or as special festival occasions. We cannot know exactly how far the churches went in dressing the miracles with "scenery"; it would probably be a matter of rich curtains and simple platforms, if indeed the producers did not realize that the altar area without change is one of the most beautiful and theatrical stages in the world. And when a little later the plays were transferred to the steps and porch before the church, could any more fitting formal stage be devised than this one with its rich cathedral-portal background, with the architectural façade rising to be lost in spires far above?

As the plays became more secular, as the Mysteries took the place of the more strictly orthodox Miracles, the theatre moved farther from the church. Temporary stages were erected for each new "cycle," and these took many forms, from the simple wooden platform on trestles with curtains at the back, to the multiple "mansion" stage with its row of built "localities." We have contemporary pictures of several examples, of which I am reproducing perhaps the most characteristic. In Fouquet's miniature painting the two-storied stage, with its several canopied compartments on the second level, indicates little by way of decoration beyond that favorite, habitual and ornate feature, "Hell-mouth." In Cailleau's miniature of the Valenciennes Passion Play of 1547, there is the typical later arrangement of long platform stage with many architectural summaries of place. Almost invariably these stages seem to have been characterized by a row of constructions beginning at the right with something called Paradise and ending at the left with the realistic Hell-mouth that could be made to belch flames. Between were the temple, Herod's house and similar localized places (as surviving even to-day on the Oberammergau Passion stage). The theory of the stage of the "simultaneous scene" is that a large stage or playing space will in the minds of the audience identify itself with any one of a number of indicated scenes if the actor enters from or begins acting at the point where the indication is given. For example, in the playing of the Herod scenes the entire stage would be used after a start had been made at the station known as Herod's house. There are records of a simultaneous-scene stage with twenty-four stations. Just how early the producers of Miracle and Mystery Plays began to introduce machinery for stage effects, and just when realistic building of the localities came in, cannot be determined; but here is a stage partly illusive, partly neutral architecture, and with curious intermingling of theatrical convention and realistic portrayal.

Special forms of the Mystery stage were those built on the three-decker system, as developed particularly in Germany, and the wagon stages utilized so extensively in England, where the guilds gave the plays in cycles, each guild presenting a scene from its own stage-car, wheeled in its turn into each of the many places where spectators gathered to see the performance. Of all the mediaeval religious "theatres," however, the only one that even moderately affected the course of stage decoration was that of the simultaneous scene. This system of staging was in effect upon the stage of the famous Hotel de Bourgogne in Paris during the early seventeenth century, as evidenced in a very interesting book of sketches still existing.

While absolute verification is lacking, there is sufficient evidence to warrant the belief that a special form of theatre developed, outside the Rome-Renaissance progression, for the plays of Terence and Plautus as acted at the schools in the fourteenth and fifteenth centuries. Manuscripts of the early fifteenth century and editions of Terence printed between 1493 and 1545 indicate the existence of a type stage formed of a projecting platform and a background of a series of arches curtained. It is a purely formal sort of stage, its decorative values arising out of the permanent design. It links neither with any well-known earlier stage nor with later developments. In the same way there are, so to speak, "fugitive" stages of simple sorts throughout this period when the drama is again finding its place in the world: the temporary erections used by strolling bands of players, the plain curtained stages of the Commedia dell' Arte as depicted by Callot, the well-remembered platform of Tabarin in Paris, the floating theatres, the early German folk stages, the farce platforms. In all of these the curtained background is a usual "decorative" feature; and at times the curtains bore patterns or pictures—the latter indicated in at least one painting by Callot and in the little woodcut I am reproducing to illustrate a German stage of the Hans Sachs period.

The so-called "tennis court theatre" in France evolved for exactly the same reason that can be assigned for the Elizabethan English theatre on the combined plan of the inn-yard and the bear-pit: the drama simply was seeking a typical "place for seeing," and a game-court was just that. The form of the place, however, contributed more to the making of the theatre auditorium than it did to determining stage form or decoration.

In the case of the Elizabethan theatre, however, the stage is of a unique sort that demands attention not only on its own account but as model for certain "modernist" stages now that there is a revolt against the eighteenth-nineteenth century picture setting. In England when the guilds no longer commonly gave the Mystery plays, the drama passed into the hands of strolling professional players, who were accustomed to set up a platform-stage in an inn-yard. The surrounding balconies served "the quality" for seats, while the "groundlings" stood below, all facing a platform at one end of the court. From this arrangement and from the bear-pit, a small arena for animal-baiting exhibitions and cock-fights, the form of Shakespeare's theatre evolved. It was in effect a high round doughnut sort of building, with the interior formed of tier upon tier of covered boxes on three sides and encroaching toward the fourth, with the pit open to the sky, and an architectural stage to complete the circle. A Dutch scholar traveled in England in 1596 and has left us the only contemporary drawing of the Elizabethan theatre. But from that and existing records of the time, it has been possible for later scholars to reconstruct the building with reasonable approach to exactness. A raised stage jutting forward into the pit from the doughnut wall, with two free columns half-way back to hold up a roof over part of the acting space; behind the platform a portion of the doughnut itself arranged with a permanent balcony above and a curtained recess below, for occasional use in discovery and transformation scenes; permanent doorways: this is, indeed, a most usable, variable and pleasing stage, with all the virtues of one architectural scene standing for all scenes, without curtain or facilities for spectacle or realism. Again the stage *is* the decoration. There is no evidence, indeed, that "scenery" was introduced to this sort of theatre even when the Italian style was being imported for court productions. When Italian settings came in, a new type of theatre came with them—and Shakespeare's playhouse disappeared with remarkable completeness.

In the low countries there was something vaguely related to these English theatres in certain playhouses of the sixteenth century, like the Rederijker Stage at Ghent (1539) and the Rederijker Stage at Antwerp (1561); and in the following century there is a real likeness in the Amsterdam theatre shown by Nicholas van Kempen in his series of views dated 1638. I am reproducing the engraving of this curious stage, truly architectural but with perspective bits and an array of "localities" reminiscent of the Mystery stages. It too, however, ultimately gave way before the novel picture stage with the proscenium frame from Italy.

Returning now to that first "modern" stage in the theatre at Parma, let us inquire just what were the settings that were to go inside the frame, hereafter to be designed and constructed afresh for each new play, even for every act of every play. The sources were certainly many; but there are two chief types of scene, and two corresponding chief impulses. On the one hand Italian artists had developed that already-mentioned passion for the re-discovered art of perspective, not only as it applied scientifically to painting but in such applications as the decoration of walls to increase apparently the size of a room; and this new plaything, fitting in so perfectly with interpretations of Vitruvius' paragraphs on the theatrical "scene," led to the clever development of perspective stage vistas. On the other hand the carnivals, pageantry and festival productions at the courts had already brought the engineer and the architect into service for the creation of spectacular "effects"—sometimes only vaguely for dramatic ends, other times for even luxuriant settings; and the engineer and architect began to call in more and more frequently the painter, who, from designing at first perhaps only the small backcloth that closed an architectural vista, gradually took over the whole stage. For a time, however, the two sorts developed side by side: imitational architectural perspective and painter's depicted scene. Since the painter does become sole master later, and therefore monopolizes practically all the rest of my story, I shall follow out the minor perspective development first. (Since we are crowding out all other types and sources for these two, I may mention just here that the popular

Commedia dell' Arte players brought along at least an influence, toward the "street" setting, when they came indoors, and that there is some relationship of pageantry to the broader show elements of the religious plays.)

The "perspective stage" was developed first on the authority and basis of Vitruvius' description of all scenography as divided into a comic scene and a tragic scene, both architectural, and a landscape satyric scene. The second volume of Sebastiano Serlio's famous *Architettura*, dealing with perspective, appeared in 1545. Therein Serlio pictured the three scenes as he understood them from Vitruvius, doubtless modified by essays in actual application of the principles to current staging; not as "decorations" for *periacti*, but each a full stage construction. His two type perspective scenes are reproduced in plate 22, and I need say no more about them here than that they had great influence on practice thereafter over most of Europe. There were soon translations of Serlio in all the chief languages, and at least one writer, Fuerttenbach, in Germany, published very interesting free adaptations of Serlio's stages.

The non-academic productions of the time were being staged almost altogether in the halls of palaces, and a stage and its scene would be built for a single production or a cycle. The many individual perspectives thus constructed went through many modifications and arrived at many variations. Certain contemporary or nearly contemporary prints, however, and written descriptions, indicate that the general characteristic of the form, a stage shaped as a diminishing street between two rows of buildings, persisted in both temporary hall-theatres and the later proscenium-frame houses. The scenes, in the true type, were built of canvas on wooden frames, in exact imitation (not portrayal) of architecture, with the relief all built out, but with the measurements lessened as the buildings receded. The backcloth closing the vista might be in painted perspective, as distinguished from the *built* perspective of the rest of the scene.

The placing of all drama in three scenes, instead of presenting all types on one formal architectural stage, was, of course, a step toward verisimilitude; but again it should be emphasized that these scenes were being developed as an attraction added to the representation of the play rather than to provide the illusion of a definite place named by a dramatist. There was as yet no conviction that a "real" scene would help to make the drama live. We are unmistakably traveling toward realistic scene-making, but have not arrived.

The perspective scene progressed, then, from wide use as "type" background, and from "set" use in a stage like that at Vicenza, to individualized use for single play and single act. The comic scene was widely utilized for the Commedia dell' Arte, for productions of Plautus and Terence, and then for comedies written specially for the festal occasions. In the latter case we know that the street was sometimes localized. Finally, of course, the current of architectural perspective setting merged almost indistinguishably with the parallel current on which the painters were riding. Before turning to that other current, I want to violate chronology again by jumping forward to consideration of the final glorification of the purely architectural scene, in the work of the famous Bibienas and their followers.

Here the setting became such a maze of columns, corridors, vistas and profuse ornament that the poor old drama had hard going to get itself seen and heard at all. The imitation architecture that had come in as an added attraction and novelty in the Vicenza theatre, that had formed pleasing stage backgrounds after the manner of Serlio, now all but crowded everything else out of the theatre. Designed presumably as a grand background for acting, these settings smothered the players in immensity and garishness. Sometimes they were architecturally very fine in the artificial manner; again they were so over-involved that anyone would mark them as downright vain display. Giovanni Maria Galli-Bibiena, the first of the line, discovered that by abandoning the single vista and the straight view, by running corridors or streets off at divergent angles, he could attain new variety, complexity and richness. What he and his sons and followers did was all that was necessary to destroy that last vestige of the feeling of serenity, enclosure and intimacy that had belonged to the old truly architectural stage, and that had to some degree characterized the earlier imitational architectural settings. Of course such "show" scenes were bound to be imitated by decorators throughout Europe; and even so recently as a decade ago a horribly involved second-rate version of a Bibiena "creation" was in use (or I might better say, on display) at the Metropolitan Opera House in New York.

If the painter trailed the architect in invading the field of theatre production, he made a fuller conquest when his turn came. In the end, even the Bibienas had nothing on him in the matter of gorgeous display. The first really painty elements in production can be traced back to certain characteristics of the masques and pageantry that had been carried into the lavish festival productions at the courts. One might go even farther back to the pageant cars and ornamented "floats" constructed for the processionals held to celebrate royal weddings, coronations, "entries," etc., and to the decorated stations along the procession routes. For these occasions the most elaborate tableau backgrounds were devised: such favorite subjects as grottoes, huge shells, dragons and bits of forest were repeated in every imaginable form. The first records of such elements in indoor production date from late in the fifteenth century; but it is said that by the early years of the sixteenth century every court in Italy had either a permanent hall-theatre or a ballroom that could on occasion be converted into curtained platform stage, dancing floor and auditorium.

The usual arrangement for this mixed transitional type of drama and theatre is indicated in Callot's etching of a masque as given at the Court of the Medici in Florence (plate 28), with a stage and spectacular scene at one end of the room, stairways or ramps leading down to the hall floor where the dances were performed, and spectators ranged in horseshoe shape around the dancing space. The engraving of the *Ballet de la Royne* (1581) is perhaps a more illuminating link between pageant or processional and theatre, because the stage here has not progressed so close to the proscenium-frame type, and the individual pageant constructions are to be seen on the dance floor. The famous court masques in England a little later were, of course, modeled on these Continental examples; and they reached the same lavishness and a like degree of spectacular display—which was all very fine in its own field, but should not perhaps have been allowed to swamp the typically dramatic play.*

* Ben Jonson, piqued because he was paid for his masque texts no more than Inigo Jones received for their staging, wrote a satire in which this line occurred: "Painting and carpentry are the soul of masque."

It is only too easy to see how the display elements, with their pleasing novelty, cleverness and prettiness, after once being brought to the stages for masques and festivals, gradually made their bid for consideration as backgrounds for the more regular drama. It seems to me clear that it was the spectacular appeal that first landed the painter's setting on the play stage, not any theory of mounting the drama in a semblance of a real place. Then somewhere along the way a producer doubtless said: "What fools we've been! Every poet *says* his action occurs in a certain described place. Why haven't we known enough to show it actually in that place?" And straightway the representation of a localized spot out of nature began to be shown—and the illusional picture setting was really born. From being presented on a neutral formal stage, often decorated but not localized, the drama was transported into a series of picture scenes. Nor has it ever escaped from the picture stage in the three centuries or so since. And the picture-frame theatre at Parma became the prototype of the later stages throughout Europe.

For convenience of discussion I have treated this development of painter's setting as along lines separate from the previously discussed "perspective" current; but in fact perspective work was woven into even the most painty creations. It survived as architectural modeled vistas for a time, but the greater ease of merely painting the whole picture militated against continued extensive use of built elements; and in the end it was painted perspective that characterized spectacular staging through most of the years following, and it was the obvious inappropriateness of painted perspective on the three-dimensional stage that provoked the ultimate twentieth-century revolt against the picture scene.

But in these early times there was no separating in practice the work of the painter from that of the architect and the engineer. Some of the earliest settings in Italy of which we have knowledge evidently combined the work of all three. Well-informed stage decorators of to-day will tell you that their present complicated stage machinery can accomplish little in the way of "effects" (except in lighting) that the Renaissance artists could not achieve with their paint and canvas and their machines developed on Roman models.

How immediately the spectacular picture setting and its "effects" came into wide popular favor is indicated in many documents of the times; and the believer in drama on its own account may have more than a just suspicion that scene-making began right there to be pursued on the general principle of putting in a lot of things to please the children. Vasari in his *Lives of the Most Eminent Painters, Sculptors and Architects,* a work of the seventeenth century, wrote: "Baldassare [Peruzzi] made two such scenes, which were marvelous, and opened the way to those who have since made them in our own day. Nor is it possible to imagine how he found room, in a space so limited, for so many streets, so many palaces, and so many bizarre temples, loggie, and various kinds of cornices, all so well executed that it seemed that they were not counterfeited, but absolutely real, and that the piazza was not a little thing, and merely painted, but real and very large. He designed, also, the chandeliers and the lights within which illumined the scene, and all the other things that were necessary, with much judgment, although, as has been related, the drama had fallen almost completely out of fashion."* The same note of wonder is evident in much of the writing of the period, and the same appreciation of the spectacular values even when the play as such attracted little attention. Vasari's last line brings up a truth that has been much bandied about in our day, notably that the time for spectacular display in settings is when the drama itself is weak.

In making use of the term "picture setting," I confess to a regrettable inexactness, in that "picture" might strictly be considered to apply only to graphic representation on a flat surface. But I have found no other term than "stage picture" for the non-architectural scene that the audience sees through the proscenium frame. It is a picture not in the flat, but with a certain depth, with space between the parts, with elements in relief—like those bastard things called "relief-paintings"—but a picture certainly in the sense of depicting a place chiefly with canvas and paint.

Passing over many intermediate steps in the progress from spectacle on its own account toward the detailed illusional setting, and the matter of the relationship between the pioneering court and private theatres and the pub-

* I have taken this quotation from Lily B. Campbell's *Scenes and Machines on the English Stage during the Renaissance* (Cambridge University Press, 1923), a treasure-house of information and old documents.

lic theatres—as also the steps in importing Italian methods into France and England, and the controversies in France over admission of spectacular elements into "regular" production—I wish to call the attention of the reader to the drawing by Cochin showing the tiny theatre built for Mme. de Pompadour in the palace at Versailles, during a production of *Acis and Galatea* (plate 32). The auditorium is depicted together with the scene on the stage, and in the contrast between the two halves of the illustration one may see just how far the setting had then traveled away from the ideal of the architectural stage. The scene is absolutely a painter's conception, with the acting platform disguised and hidden. The actors have become hardly more than incidental figures in an easel-picture.

Three other reproductions illustrate the same point: the masque setting by Inigo Jones is equally painter-like in conception; and the two theatres with settings illustrated in plate 33 indicate how completely the stage of the larger playhouse was lost to sight and a framed picture presented to the view of the audience.

Of course the stage picture did not always, or often, appear as perfect as these engravings would lead one to believe; indeed, in the eighteenth and nineteenth centuries, after the "wing" settings had come into common use, if there were any architectural elements in the scene the lines were likely to be askew as seen from any but one point in the auditorium. As methods of changing settings developed (the first picture scenes were individual creations, too cumbersome to permit change), and as standardization of units became necessary, the decorators developed a mechanical system of back-drop and "wing-pieces." These latter were easily removable screen pieces, made of canvas on wooden frames, that could be fastened on poles sliding in grooves off and on stage; and in the normal setting, rows of these towering painted screens, reaching from floor to ceiling-borders, and set parallel to the front curtain and backcloth, flanked the acting space. Toward the front the wings were set wider apart, so that the free stage area had much the same shape as in the older diminishing perspective scene—like a V with the sharp angle cut off by the back-drop. The "borders" closing the view at the top were a series of cloth strips, hung one behind another until the entire "top works" between proscenium and drop was cut off from the view of spectators in the front row of seats. From one point in the auditorium the lines of the architecture painted on one wing-piece matched perfectly with that on the next piece behind, but from any point to right or left of this key-seat there was an evident discrepancy. Under the little-controlled lighting, too, the edges of the wings showed up in over-emphasis. The effect obtained was more often like that shown in the little cut opposite plate 34 than like the ideally articulated scenes commonly shown in reproductions. But the audiences—who by this time were considered incapable of accepting the convention of a formal stage standing for all scenes—came to accept the lack of real illusion in the wing scenes as "theatrical."

For a very long time the wing set served for practically all exteriors and interiors; and (except on the "apron") there were no doorways to the stage, only space between the wings. The setting of the screen scene of *The School for Scandal* at Drury Lane Theatre is typical, with its window and bookcase painted on the backcloth, and its architectural elements represented in paint on wings slid in on the two sides of the playing space. Here a feature of the formal stage has persisted in the large undecorated forestage, or apron, with its permanent portals. As the scenic tradition ran down, it was a common practice to paint on the walls all furniture not actually used during the performance. In vaudeville theatres to-day, you may run across the typical wing setting, without side walls, and occasionally you may even see painted-in furniture in addition to the painted mantels and low architectural relief.

When the theatres began to be built with high stage lofts, more than twice as high as the proscenium opening, the disillusioning regularity of the wing-rows came to be broken by wider use of "hanging stuff." This consisted of "leg-drops," oblique pieces, porches, fountains, and the like, that could be "flied" when not in use and as easily let down into the scene when called for. The oblique pieces (not in the grooves) were, of course, a step toward the later box set interior. A great deal of stage setting was by this time being accomplished by rigid rule, and often according to a convenient classification of palace set, kitchen set, garden set, drawing-room, etc.—a step back toward Serlio's type scenes, indeed! A theatre just opening could order in from the scenic studio a half dozen stock scenes; and if its flying-space and its storage space for flats were ample enough to store all at once, it would have on the premises a complete decorative equipment, sufficient with a little ingenuity for every need. By common usage a shorthand reference system developed, so that a playwright simply noted: "Sc. 2—an elegant apartment, 4 and 7G. French windows in flat R and L. Lattice C doors open, backed with garden flats. Garden cloth down from 4th to 7th G. painted with walks and flower beds. Set statues, flower pieces . . ." And the scene was easily made up from the drawing-room set and the garden set. A similar convention, of course, applied to actors: first and second lead, female lead, juvenile, adventuress, soubrette, villain, etc. All this routining and skimping of theatre materials, of course, had its effect on playwriting, so that most of the nineteenth century was a sterile period in the history of world drama—or was it that sterile and routine drama produced lifeless and careless setting?

At the other extreme of decoration there were marvelously careful attempts to build up plausible magnificence, with a clever blending together of practicable units in the foreground and painted perspective beyond (plates 36 and 37). If the producer had enough money at his command, he could cause to be built and painted almost exact duplicates of real palace halls and church interiors. He thus, in the imitation of show places, created natural settings some decades before naturalism as a creed came in (plate 38). In exterior scenes a sort of painter's romantic naturalism came into style in the nineteenth century; and if any reader should see an apparent contradiction in the description, let him study the *Parsifal* forest of plate 39. Still it cannot justly be said that the painters ever gave a true and complete illusion of a forest except on a somewhat dark stage.

In the end, indeed, the painted picture setting, which came to the dramatic stage first as an added element of spectacle and then as an attempt to depict the locality chosen by the dramatist for his action, failed to add to the truly dramatic values with its spectacle, and proved itself able at its best only to approximate actuality and at its worst to afford a tawdry and artificial caricature of reality. In the late nineteenth century the great tradition of scene painting had so badly run down in most places that nine out of ten plays were being presented in settings not only tasteless and untheatrical (in the best sense of "theatrical") but ridiculously artificial, muddy in color and without evidence of a knowledge of elementary picture composition. Where the grand manner still persisted the actor was surrounded with acres of painted magnificence that dwarfed him and injured the play as such. It was against the perpetrators of this double failure, in negligent artificiality and in unrelated painter's elaboration, that the battle cry of the naturalists was hurled in the 'nineties.

At this time the stage was a huge box with a curtained peep-hole opening in the front. When the curtain was raised the audience looked into a stage flanked by canvas wings, appearing frankly in rows as such, or with hinged flaps for variety or as "cut-outs" supplementing "leg-drops" and "set pieces" in an effort toward a painty sort of reality. Scene painting had had glories of its own—but the world was beginning to question whether painting had ever really belonged on the stage of the essential acted drama.

# III

## NATURALISM

WHAT is sometimes questionably termed the first modern revolt in methods of staging occurred in the late years of the nineteenth century. Noting the ridiculous artifice and fake of the pictures in which the plays, not only of the old artificial dramatists but of the current realistic playwrights, pretending to truth above all else, were being presented, a few producers and directors here and there set about to make the backgrounds more reasonable and more natural. The leaders in this progressive work were Otto Brahm in Europe and David Belasco in America, and Antoine was its pioneer in France.

The revolt, if such it may be called, was purely in the interests of naturalism. It achieved a fresh appropriateness of play and setting, but it marked only the final reach of realism, the ultimate photographic achievement at the end of a centuries-old obsession with the observed thing, with imitation of the surface of life, with the truthfulness of casual detail, as distinguished from the search to be made later for the living spirit, imaginative, emotional and formal qualities. This first reach forward is seen now as important in the aspect of a clearing of the ground, but the type of setting it developed is in itself as unfitted to to day's theatre and to-day's drama as the thing it dethroned, and almost as ridiculous and distracting. It was the stage parallel to that achievement in painting by which each hair of the cow's hide was made apparent separately, and each leaf of the tree depicted with exactitude.

Brahm was busy with the staging of Ibsen and other giants of realism, whereas Belasco had somewhat watered material to inspire his inventiveness. But about the same time both became convinced that the setting must be made of a piece with the "slice-of-life" drama. This consideration led them first to banish such absolute unnaturalnesses as furniture painted on the room walls and loosely flapping painted scene drops in landscapes. From this it was a natural progression to the observation that painted shadows seldom accorded with true shadows, seldom could be matched with the actual sources of light. Up to this time the mouldings, door-frames and other low relief in the stage room had been almost universally painted on to the walls, under an ancient convention of shadowing. This noticeably artificial makeshift was abolished, and actual mouldings, door-frames, mantels and window-frames were brought into the scene. At the same time the walls were made more solid, so that the canvas "flats" of which they were constructed no longer quaked at the slightest touch. Where doors had flourished before in unnatural profusion, one or two reasonable doorways were now seen to be enough—and more natural. The property man, who had long exercised his ingenuity, fancy and taste, if any, in furnishing the stage room, according to a convenient classification of palace sets, kitchen sets, etc., was now restrained; the clutter of unrelated ornamental and useful pieces was cleared out, and such furniture put in as might be found in a real room in a real house of the period. The producer might even send over to the theatre a suite of his own, to be sure it was actual used and usable stuff.

If the business had stopped there, and then if a little real taste had been exercised, the change would have represented an immense and permanent gain. For the scene had been stripped of its ridiculously false trappings, a lot of things wrongly inherited from opera and magnificently romantic drama had been discarded, and a new solidity and material correctness had been achieved. But the artists of the Belasco school of naturalism were aiming at a scene as full of display in its way as the operatic sort had been in its way. They wanted nothing less than a scene that would come out and *proclaim* that it was real.

They developed a philosophy of "the importance of the little things," and in an attempt to portray actual rooms with absolute photographic perfection, they brought into the setting a profusion of casual objects. They thought that by assembling enough correct little things they could achieve truth. The actor who before had played in settings negligently and tawdrily built up with whatever the scene painter and property man found easiest to bring in, or in scenes gorgeously built up with mountains of unrelated magnificence, now found himself in a scene a-glitter with naturalistic detail, self-consciously proclaiming itself a real room by virtue of its ability to exhibit real books in real bookcases, real hat-racks with real hats on them, real phonographs and newspapers and telephones, vistas of real plants through real windows, real paneled doors, and a hundred added real accidentals as observed by the producer in lived-in rooms.

Thus one went to the theatre partly to marvel at meticulously portrayed museum examples of contemporary living-rooms, libraries and brothels. And to make the marvel more enduring, the producer added certain "effects," not of the old spectacular sort, but ingeniously true to life. Thus one remembers the two clocks in the same setting, striking the hour many seconds apart, as they actually would in your home or mine (a bit that secured newspaper attention from coast to coast); the second complete room, beyond that in which the action is passing, opened to view to beguile the audience with a sudden glimpse of a completely furnished den or a family at table, "as if one were actually in a house"; the perfectly imitated squeak of a pneumatic elevator, so perfectly imitated that every spectator turned to his neighbor to comment on the marvel. And when the play's locale was an operating room in a hospital, or the composing room of a newspaper, or a Childs' Restaurant, there was no limit to what the producer might introduce by way of satisfying curiosity about surgical machinery or linotype machines or how the other half eats.

All of which, of course, is hardly better than pandering in the name of art to humanity's craving for novelty and its enjoyment of perfect and elaborate imitation. Originating in a desire to rid the stage and play of the distractions of a ridiculous artificiality, the movement toward naturalism in settings ended in burying the action amid numberless distractions of its own sort. In the naturalistic scene there was no more aid to the essential drama than in the nineteenth century wing set, no more art—only actuality transferred and exploited. It was still the picture of a setting that was built up, and not yet even a simplified atmospheric picture.

And yet there was this net gain toward the next revolution: the painted shadows that never corresponded to the actual shadows were banished from the scene, the painted perspective that seldom matched up with the actual perspective of the pictured scene was laughed out of existence, and in general the worst excesses of the traditional scene *painter* were put aside for all time; the box-set interior, if too profusely detailed, was made solid and after a fashion honest, and a general material rightness was achieved—a rightness that afforded a real foundation for creative work by those who came in turn to strip the stage room again, and to "decorate" not realistically and profusely, but with restraint and taste.

The naturalistic development, as a matter of fact, never quite satisfied its own most devoted practitioners in the matter of certain problems arising in the staging of outdoor scenes. A forest scene, for instance, was difficult and expensive to set with real trees; and the painted sort, no matter how carefully each leaf was depicted in accordance with nature, somehow always afforded a feeling of second-rate trees, not quite alive. The larger and finer the scene called for by the author, the more meager seemed the "fiction of reality" achieved by the stage artist.

In the matter of indoor settings, the realists developed "the convention of the fourth wall." That is, they decreed that playwrights should write their plays exactly as if they were looking into a room from which the side wall next them had been removed (without being noticed by the characters within); and many were the devices used by the scenic artists to convey this conception visibly to the audiences. A favorite indication of the missing fourth side of the room was a set of andirons placed down toward the footlights, with actors coming to it every little while to warm their hands at a fire which presumably had been removed with the wall. In the very act of removing the wall, of course, in adopting a convention, the realists confessed the weakness of their creed, and foreshadowed the collapse of the entire system of writing and production developed by them. For it is true that the nearer to perfection an imitation comes, the less value it has on its own account; on the stage, the moment the point arrives where the spectator exclaims "How lifelike that is!" the dramatic web is broken. Ultimately the dramatist or the scenic worker reaches the impasse created by his own skill and has to adopt a convention—some device which in itself carries the confession that this after all is not nature but a work of artifice.

The realists became even more strongly entrenched in the theatres in the last years of the century than the "old style" artists had been a decade or two earlier. The fight for naturalism in setting as in playwriting had been won only after a bitter and prolonged struggle, and most of the world of the theatre had come to look on realism as on a religion. (The realists objected to the term "naturalism," although their imitativeness was exact enough to warrant the name; naturalism being in my definition the ultimate point in realism, not only emphasis on the observed fact as against revelation of spirit and beauty of form, but exploitation of imitation on its own photographic account, and glorification of accidental detail.)

But a new generation of insurgents was growing up, with two giant figures to nurture them with a different ideal, two artists greater than any developed under the realistic banner: Gordon Craig and Adolphe Appia. These later progressives not only doubted that realism was a final achievement on the stage; they came forward with a definite conviction that although the setting might be literally correct according to the playwright's directions, with just the number of doors and windows needed, and the right properties not too many times multiplied, it would never fulfill its whole duty by mere material conformance: scale in the setting, design of the parts, and possibly something called style might serve art and the stage better. One practitioner after another reflected that after all art is in itself a convention. And had not many a philosopher commented on the great gap existing between the exact and the true?

# IV

## THE TASTE FOR REALISTIC SETTINGS

THE simplifying and making tasteful of the realistic setting, the dressing of contemporary plays in appropriate and often lovely scenic clothes, the development of machinery to make quick and plausible the passing of the scenes before the eye, and particularly the advance in lighting efficiency, affording not a little atmospheric beauty—these changes, accomplished in the last twenty-five years in innumerable theatres, and capitalized more for the setting forth of a dying type of play than in the service of any emerging new drama, constitute for most observers *the* modern revolution in stage decoration. As a matter of fact, the notable improvement in current practice since 1900 has been in most theatres only a surface change. The deeper revolution that is still developing in the theatre, the fundamental upheaval that aims at nothing less than the overthrow of all phases of realism after a reign extending through centuries, the change that parallels the progress toward an accepted modernism in the other arts, promises to go far beyond this general dressing-up of realistic plays or atmospheric aid to the realistic staging of old plays.

But the surface change in the better realistic playhouses during the last quarter-century is in itself a phenomenon worth intensive study, if only because it brought prettiness and light and grace where those qualities seldom existed before. The movement affords a perfect parallel to Impressionism in painting, which, despite its apparently revolutionary character at first, proved in the end to be only a special phase of realistic painting, depending upon observation of an evanescent aspect of surface reality, an immediate "effect" of nature, but nature and observation nevertheless. Impressionism in easel painting brought in fresh coloring, and love of light, and freedom from over-detailing, despite its shallowness; and just about as much can be said justly for "the new stage decoration" of 1900-1925.

When Gordon Craig and Adolphe Appia came to the theatre in the years just before the close of the old century, they foreshadowed—nay, they instigated—that true revolutionary struggle that is only half fought out even to-day. They never compromised with realism, nor did they ever counsel their followers to do so. And yet they are responsible indirectly for that minor revolution within realistic limits which has brought the bulk of the world's theatres to a pretty form of Impressionistic stage setting.

Craig and Appia, clear-sighted theorists, prophets, and both endowed with a gift for written expression, were also practical artists of the stage when opportunity came to practice without compromise. Because they would not accept cramping conditions, because they would not exploit the most obvious virtues of a new art expression unless they were given opportunity to go back to beginnings and build on a wholly new foundation, they were driven to work largely in by-paths and at times in the wilderness, far from the market-place playhouses. Though they have wielded an enormous influence by means of their writings, and their ideas that have been repeated up and down the world in many languages, they themselves have pretty much stayed aloof from the contemporary stage—because that stage is designed primarily for the exhibition of realism, and is controlled by those who have never seen a vision beyond realism.

But the followers of Appia and Craig practically all took the more reasonable path, as the less extreme artist and the lesser prophet take it. They were fired with the new idea, stung with Craig's provocative urge to be up and doing in the theatre—and they turned to the only theatre at hand. In compromising as their teachers had refused to do, they were not necessarily betraying a trust, or dragging down something fine. They were merely clothing something less noble in clothes that would become nobility. Because the current drama was overwhelmingly realistic, and because they wanted to work on the only existing stages, they conveniently forgot the more extreme of the Craig-Appia teachings and set out to apply practically the more obvious ones. And be it said at once, they did a beautiful job within the limitations.

Because the ideas of the two giant figures were thus compromised in so much that has been done more or less in their name, I am leaving discussion of their personal service and their deeper philosophy until later, when we shall come to the really modernist stages, to the experiments of those who have been true to anti-realism. Just now I am setting out to show how the naturalist stage setting within the proscenium frame was changed gradually to a simplified, tasteful and often restful picture that added to the play's appeal and did not too seriously take attention from the actor.

An artist of even the keenest understanding, after seeing an exhibition of Craig's designs, and reading such of Craig's and Appia's books as were available fifteen years ago, might turn to the theatre saying: "*Unity* is the great thing. To gain unity in the whole production we can help by clearing out the useless clutter on the stage. Simplify the setting, and then do everything possible to make the actor the center of the picture." There is sound principle here, and even so little seemed then to afford a basis for an entirely different form of production.

The idea of simplification, as a means to greater unity, had a double importance. It could be used both in opposition to the flagrantly naturalistic setting, the over-detailed real picture, and to any survivals of the earlier display staging. Simplification was a weapon against elaboration of any sort, natural, romantic, archaeological or painty. "Don't choke the eye," said one designer. Another, who saw farther, perhaps, wrote that "a good simple imitation temple is better than a bad involved one." Instead of the carefully documented scene, one must build up a serviceable outline of a place, with restraint and a "technique of intimation." The structure and the machinery of the naturalistic stage and setting could be retained. But the surface must be stripped.

Simplification, applied in any mature art, is likely to prove beneficial. But it soon turns out that simplicity alone is not enough. That a stage picture is unpretentious, that it is characterized by elimination of the inessential and the undramatic, is only a negative virtue. So, beyond unity and simplification, the record of progress is marked at intervals by the employment of a series of more positive catchwords—in approximately this order: mood, synthesis, suggestion, design, the plastic, stylization.

If the merely simplified setting was not wholly right, though the material details were correct, it was easy to see that what it lacked was the intangible thing called mood. This subtler quality might hide the bareness. Progress in this direction was the easier because the lighting equipment of the stage was becoming immeasurably more flexible and capable, and the quality of light more sensitively expressive. The old lighting had been able to set out clearly a number of literal facts about a place, but the newer lighting made it possible almost to project the atmosphere of it, without stressing exact locality or material detail. The little things as well as the big could be softened and faded off into dimness. Specific interest was thus subordinated to evocation of mood. But it became apparent that "mood" was a word not for a thing visual and decorative alone but to designate the whole feeling of a production, play as well as background. And perhaps the best thing that came out of the discussion of mood was that it led to the question of achieving a synthesis of all the elements of production.

In my opening paragraphs on theory I wrote enough about synthesis as an ideal. It was during the talk about synthetic methods that the decorators generously stepped down saying: "Our work above all else must be subordinate to one man's conception of the whole production, play, scene, lighting, action. There must be perfect coördination of all emotional appeals, to the eye as well as to the ear." They began to recognize as never before that anything they might achieve was valueless theatrically unless directly and emotionally related to an artist-director's scheme and vision of the production, that the written play itself was only an incomplete expression of the art of the theatre, that the acting of it in unsympathetic surroundings was only a corruption of the dramatist's intended whole; and finally that the synthesis of the three elements, play, acting and setting, alone could be considered a complete realization of the art of the theatre. The keynote of everything must be found in the dramatist's script, and the conception of the means for carrying the flow of action through in harmony must be found in the regisseur. The decorator must serve these two—while in a different physical sense serving the actor. A theory was even developed that every truly theatrical play has in itself an art value over and above the literary, acting and spectacular values, and that the grasping of this architectonic thing in the play, its projection on the stage, is the chief work of the regisseur, and to contribute to its realization the only work of the decorator. Here one has the basis for the sayings that the decorator must work only with "an answering mind" or only to "complete the thought" of the dramatist and director.

Mood and synthesis were vague words, offering no clue to principles for immediate application to the visual problem. "Suggestion" offered more for the working decorator to hold to. As a matter of fact, it is equally vague unless one knows what it is that is to be suggested; but the designers found a good toe-hold in it because they were dealing with realistic plays, and could immediately set out to make settings suggestive of reality. Simplicity had degenerated to bareness when pursued for its own sake; but simplification could be put to work constructively if the artist exercised a nice discrimination in selecting suggestive details out of nature: a tree for a forest, a rug and a throne against a tapestry for the king's audience hall, a desk for an office.

It might even be carried further. In the old days, if a play called for a scene before the pyramids of Egypt, the scene painter, nothing daunted, had looked up some books about Egypt and painted a scene with gigantic if not wholly convincing pyramids. According as his training had been altogether in the scenic studios or partly at the art academies, he produced either a really terrible, muddied, sign-painter's caricature of grandeur, or a landscape not at all bad—but wholly untheatric in either case. In this later period of simplicity and intimation, however, at least one designer properly despaired of ever *depicting* the pyramids. So he cleared out the scene just as far as the playwright's directions would permit, and threw the shadow of a pyramid over it. The play and the actors were thus unobtrusively served with an unassuming suggestion of the background they needed. Adolphe Appia in his later work, when his stage and setting were hardly more than a floor and a wall, adopted the same device and threw the shadow of a tree across the scene.

The more usual and concrete means of suggestion is, however, to let a single Gothic pillar or arch stand for a church, a flat wall and noble doorway for a palace, a cramped room and steep stairway for a cellar. Thus may the illusion of grandeur be evoked, or of meanness; the atmosphere of tragic largeness, of sentimental laziness, of soaring aspiration.

When one simplifies *tastefully*, one unconsciously employs design and composition. Pictorial design or architectural design may be utilized to make the setting itself harmonious, graceful, restful. Beyond that there is use for the principles of pictorial composition for sheerly dramatic effectiveness. Thus in a memorable setting for *The Devil's Garden*, the designer placed a prisoner in a single isolated chair, balanced by a group of investigating officials about a desk—on the elementary yard-arm principle. Indeed, the eye of the spectator may be led to rest at any point in the scene as demanded by the dramatist's directions or the regisseur's conception. Through poor design the spectator's eye will be drawn out of the picture, as in those settings where side windows open on compelling vistas, or his gaze will be drawn restlessly back and forth by separated and opposing points of interest. Or by cunning design, his attention can be concentrated on the central playing space. All the principles of scale, proportion, contrast, balance and pictorial rhythm are applicable here.

The stage designer thus brought design to aid him after he had stripped the scene for simplification, and had chosen the few essential and characteristic motives or properties for suggestion. He arranged the scene as carefully as a painter lays out his lines and masses on his canvas. The setting became truly a pictorial decoration, and not merely a representation of a place. Another asset of the painter, color, was utilized as never before. The whole gamut of aids that we have been discussing have a color application as well as a line-and-form application: color simplification, color suggestion, color composition. And in those more intangible fields of mood and atmosphere, color psychology, color quality and color harmony came to have unexampled importance. By the delicacy, the intimation, of the pervading color, the designer could affect the spectator subconsciously; by his understanding of colors under light, he built settings into a loveliness of aspect beyond the dreams of other generations. The fullness of color of a play as set and directed by Robert Edmond Jones in New York, or by Pirchan and Jessner in Berlin, is likely to leave in retrospect a memorable overtone—as if the action had passed to the accompaniment, hardly noticed at the time, of a color symphony.

There has been more than a little confusion recently over the cry that the stage above all else must be *plastic*. When the term first began to be used in connection with decoration, it meant hardly more than that the designer used real properties and real low relief in his settings, instead of painting these things on the canvas. Gradually it came to be applied as a designation for the whole movement away from the painted perspective setting, away from the stage decorated according to the easel painter's conception and methods, and toward a more solidly architectural—a plastic setting. It does not, however, as generally used, mean a truly architectural or formal stage. If a designer discards painted perspective and painted shadows, if he no longer paints a semblance of the scene called for by the playwright, and paints no objects *on* the canvas, he is conceiving the setting plastically. That is, his canvases stretched on frames, the "flats," appear as one side of a solid, instead of being painted with a picture representing two sides. There is a somewhat difficult distinction here, in that the total setting is still being conceived indubitably as a picture, a stage picture within a proscenium frame, whereas the properties in it and the walls, pillars, stairs, etc., are set in plastically. The downright plastic stage, of course, is a wholly architectural or sculptural affair, as the stage of Jacques Copeau at the *Vieux Colombier* is architectural, and Norman-Bel Geddes' stages (as seen in models) for *Dante* and *The Mother of Christ* are sculptural. In these cases the stage, the platform for acting, is itself *in the round,* not merely the things placed on it.

The whole theory of the plastic setting is based on the unchallengeable fact that the actor always appears in the round, and therefore a pictured background on the wall or walls behind him will always be out of consonance with his presence.

To simplify the scene, to suggest far more than was shown, to utilize plastic materials, to apply laws of composition in both line-and-mass and in color—all this still left something to be desired, even in the realistic picture. That something was finally found in stylization.

## V

## STYLIZATION

STYLE is an intangible, almost indescribable thing that is added to a picture or a work of architecture or a stage setting out of the artist's creative talent, a sustained decorative treatment that lies in his individual manner of conception and working, a quality that distinguishes his solution of a given artistic problem from the solution of any other artist. Stylization implies in the beginning a harmony of the settings with the essential spirit or "tone" of the play, and after that a harmony of the various settings throughout the production; and above that is a sustained quality, a likeness in the sort of visual beauty throughout.

When an earlier generation of designers undertook to present classic dramas in settings and costumes archaeologically correct down to the last detail, they were taking a step toward stylization of a hard, dry sort. They thought to unify the play by studious application of a style out of history. They doubtless gained something toward singleness of impression thereby. But that impression was not truly emotional or intrinsically artistic.

The motif of the visual stylization may sometimes be very obvious in the production as seen on the stage. Thus I once witnessed a performance which I believe was stylized out of someone's feeling that regal red plush summed up the spirit of the period of the play's action. A designer may stylize out of an architectural peculiarity of a certain time, or out of the shape of the ladies' skirts, or out of lavender and old lace. Stylization may, of course, be drawn out of something not primarily visual; it may find its origin in a feeling for certain music that would befit this particular play, or out of a theory of a certain formality of gesture, or out of a particular rhythm in the spoken words—and in this case the designer's contribution is a running visual equivalent for the original feeling. It may be, of course, that the life of the play's period was rococo, so that a reminiscently rococo stylization would be the only right method. The designer's conception of his settings, in short, may arise out of an external detail or out of a suggestion of the author, or out of a feeling conveyed by the text—but appropriate to the play it must always be, and sustained throughout the production. It is, in a sense, a harmonic conventionalization made creative by the individual genius of the designer.

An external form of stylization, drawn from the art of painting, is that which imposes on a play a series of settings designed after a well-known manner, such as that of Whistler or of Beardsley, or that of the Munich posteresque painters. Such an alien style seldom helps the drama, although it may divert the attention and give a minor independent pleasure briefly. But the actors and action seldom fit back restfully into it. Many of the recent attempts to accomplish Cubistic and Expressionistic staging have involved nothing more than a transfer of the principles of modernist painting to one element of the production, the settings, leaving the play and acting untouched and unrelated. In stylizing his work at all, be it added, the scene designer is only belatedly catching up with progress in the other arts; but borrowing from them direct has not helped his case.

At its worst, stylization on the stage may thus be an imposition of a thing borrowed or stolen unreasonably; at its best it is an addition as a part of the regisseur's plan and a completion of the dramatist's intention.

The first examples of practical stylization that were brought widely to the notice of the world were doubtless conceived primarily as pictorial decoration and not theatrically. The startlingly simple, posteresque and colorful stage pictures that Emil Orlik and Ernst Stern designed for Max Reinhardt's productions are likely to seem now a trifle heavily decorative; the Shakespearean performances directed by Granville Barker in scenes by Norman Wilkinson and Albert Rutherston, delicate and enchanting as they were, seem a little like transfers from story-book illustration; and the settings which Jacques Rouché induced leading French insurgent painters to do for his productions at the *Théâtre des Arts* between 1910 and 1913 now can be judged as interesting instances of newly found styles in painting being brought bodily to the stage. The Viennese decorator, the easel painter who was rediscovering conventionalization and structure after the debauch of formlessness incident to early Impressionism, the rediscoverers of peasant art, and the lush oriental decorators, all had a hand at improving the scene.

Among my illustrations I have tried to include chiefly examples that illustrate typically theatrical stylization, but traces of these various transferred methods can doubtless be found. I have carefully covered the field, however, so far as varying types of play are concerned, plates 54 to 66 ranging through opera, romantic play and realistic pieces.

The difficulties of stylization, and the failures after honest effort, can usually be traced to failure sufficiently to consider the actor (granted that the play script itself does not contain the seeds of disintegration and discord); the designer finds his chief pitfall where lies the opportunity for a display of style not strictly in accord with the postulate that the player must dominate the scene. There is one form of contemporary production, however, in which the artist has found latitude for a show of virtuosity without injury to the essential action. In the dance-drama the perfect opportunity for a gorgeous sensuous stylization has been found.

In the forms developed by the *Ballets Russes* particularly, decoration has a more positive function than in the truly dramatic forms. Color plays an enormous part, pretentious and stirring scenery aids rather than detracts from the total effect; in short, the director leans heavily on all sensuous aids. There is no close-knit story of which the spell may be broken by a "loud" setting, no dialogue to be favored with quietness and intimately hushed surroundings.

The appeal of the dance-drama is primarily by sight and by abstract sound —music. The effect is compounded out of color and line used creatively, movement and music. It is an art that aims at intoxication of the senses. The synthesis here is of all sensuous elements, with the intellect and all that addresses it stilled. The stylization oftener than not arises out of a conception of a gorgeous picture or a color or a visual effect. The painter becomes not the servant of an author and director, but fellow-creator.

Leon Bakst, the acknowledged master of the dance-drama setting, once wrote: "Nowadays it is the painter who, taking the place of the erudite director, should create everything, know everything, foresee and organize everything. It is the painter who must be master of the situation, understand its finesse, subtleties, and decide the style of the piece; to his plastic judgment and taste must be subordinated the thousand details which are combined in the imposing ensemble of a great work of the theatre." In this spirit Bakst and his fellow artists, Benois, Roerich, Golovine and Anisfeld picked up the old painted-perspective scene, glorified its painty virtues and defects, and transformed the whole with an amazing richness of color and sweep of line. They built, out of painted canvas, scenes that outdid in bigness, voluptuousness and lusciousness anything ever seen on canvas before. Red and green simply played their way through the passionate *Sheherazade*, and reds, oranges and yellows kept *Thamar* intense throughout.

This achievement of an orientally rich stylization with paint had little to do with the sort of theatre dreamed by Craig and Appia. Nor did it link up with the work of that larger group of designers who thought they were realizing the new theatre by dressing the current drama tastefully. These Russian Ballet people forgot simplicity and suggestion, they utilized painted perspective, and often enough they piled up mountains of scenery. The truth of the matter is simply this: Bakst developed a gorgeous technique for the sort of drama that lies in one little corner of the field of theatre aesthetics, and outside that field, in any other sort of play, his designs would seem an intrusion, garish, overwhelming.

Those of us who have found a thrilling, at times an ecstatic pleasure in the intense dance-drama and its sumptuous scenes are inclined to find agreeable on rare occasions another sort of exaggeration that similarly involves a transfer from the graphic arts. When a primarily fantastic play is to be clothed, the most successful sort of stylization seems to be that which approximates contemporary fairy-book illustration. The highly conventionalized treatment and the sweetly delicate coloring seem to add to the sentimental mood of most so-called fantastic writers. Just how wide is the gap between fantasy and direct imaginative reach (as in Shakespeare so often), we need not inquire here. For fantasy as we have it, a Rackham drawing seems right.

One of the finest and perhaps the best-known example is the Moscow Art Theatre's mounting of Maeterlinck's *The Blue Bird*, as conceived by the director Stanislavsky and painted by Egoroff. It is strictly a graphic artist's method of picture making that is imposed on the play, but here is such a wealth of pretty decorativeness, so much that fits in visually with the sentimental other-worldliness of the text, that one must find the "spread" of the settings enriching rather than disturbing. Perhaps it is because usually fantasy as written for the stage partakes of a literary sort of imaginativeness, rather than theatric reaches, that the illustrative setting so befits it. It is in any case, of course, outside the main stream of progress in stagecraft.

It is but a short step from this sort of conventionalization to purely symbolic setting—if there can be such a thing in the theatre. A symbol, in its most direct definition, is something that stands for something else, a thing that stands for more than itself. It is clear, then, that as soon as an artist begins to exercise a selective sense, to make the setting suggestive rather than literal, he is traveling toward the use of symbolism, if not accomplishing it in some degree. How far he must go actually to arrive as a symbolist, I do not know. And though I have heard of settings in which a device on a curtain was made to act as a symbol for all the facts of a scene, I am unable to put my hand on any picture that will illustrate the point—nor is my memory clear about any example. It seems to me that the progression from literal to suggestive settings will ultimately carry the artist toward abstraction rather than toward symbolism—though I doubt that either can be achieved in an absolute sense. So far the talk about symbolism as a chief aim of modern stage decoration has only proved confusing. Either one has a certain amount of conventionalization within the reasonably realistic picture, or one goes flatly over to Expressionistic means.

# VI

## THE PROGRESS IN MECHANICS AND LIGHTING

ACCOMPANYING at first the progress toward naturalness, and then that toward appropriateness of setting, between 1895 and 1920, there was a steady gain in the mechanical means toward ease and flexibility of scene-shifting and lighting. The machinery of the stage was developed to a marvelous efficiency, and the lighting equipment became a delicate and intricate instrument on which an artist could play a sensitive accompaniment to the dramatic action.

In the days before naturalism the scenic designers had developed an amazing array of machinery for rearing vast edifices of scenery and for trick effects. When the settings had become so elaborate that it took twenty minutes and half an hour between scenes to accomplish a change, a new sort of stage mechanics became necessary, to permit the scenes to be brought before the eye more rapidly.

*A "wing" setting, from behind.*

The older stage was a fairly open box-like space, with floor sloping down slightly toward the auditorium, pierced with a proscenium opening less than half as high as the roof of the box, and approximately one half as wide as the greatest stage width; within this rectangular space, the portion looked into by the audience was flanked on each side by rows of "wings" made to slide on or off stage in grooves, and it was closed at the back by a painted "drop"—one of many immense painted curtains hanging above and ready to be let down from the gridiron; and the top space was cut off from the eye by succeeding narrow strips called "borders." An "apron" might extend the front of the stage considerably before the curtain line. This stage was lighted almost entirely by footlights and a few border lights placed just inside the top edge of the proscenium arch and perhaps down its sides, and possibly by strips in the wings.

With the adoption of the box-set scene, the setting began to be made of independent and free-moving "flats" (canvas pieces stretched over light wooden frames) lashed together at the back with rope. When an interior

scene was set, it had the appearance of a small box constructed of canvas on a wooden frame, set within the larger permanent box that was the stage-building. The wings were gone, there was less hanging stuff overhead, and the borders had disappeared except for emergency use. When the scene was "struck," the ceiling, really a huge screen hinged into two or more pieces, was pulled up, folding on the hinged edge; the ropes were unlashed and the sections or "flats" were drawn by stagehands along the floor like towering screens, to resting places against the walls or in racks. The grooves disappeared—they were useless now because the side walls of the box scene cut directly across them—the slope was taken out of the stage floor, and the size of the proscenium opening was cut down to provide more strategic positions for border lights and for individual spot and flood lights. (The drawing of a simple box setting as sketched by Ernst Stern on Reinhardt's stage indicates both the method of putting together the flats, and the manner of building the setting in open space rather than with slid-in wings. I am adding also an exterior scene of a slightly earlier vintage, of the intermediate period when the parallel wings had disappeared, but with borders above and a painted backcloth. It may serve to remind the reader that although I jump from type to type, there was evolutionary change, with many mixed examples between.)

The comparative immensity of the stage was characteristic of theatres built during the naturalistic period as it was during the era of display settings, and this immensity more or less persists to-day. In plate 39 is a reproduction of a "section" of the Paris Opera House, built just at the end of the "old style" period, to show the large ramped stage in relation to the auditorium, the litter of hanging scenery, the stage maze of operating balconies and stairways, and the necessary two floors of machinery over the stage space and the six floors below. How far had we come then from the Greek platform for acting! And how far from continuous action!

One of the earliest devices to hasten change of scene was the revolving stage. This invention, in use in Japan before Europe and America discovered its potentialities, allowed the designer to set three, four or even five full scenes at one time, to be rolled before the proscenium opening in turn when needed. The revolving turn-table occupies, of course, only the center portion of the stage space, being wider than the proscenium opening, touching approximately the curtain line at the front of its circumference, and leaving at the back and sides ample working space. Before the first rise of the curtain the four or five scenes are set up with flats, cut-outs and properties complete, each scene being either a small box-set just wide and high enough to fill the proscenium opening, or partly open and devised in such a way that the eye of the spectator in looking up and off beyond it encounters only an architectural or wooded vista or a cyclorama drop farther back on the stage. This circular platform, bearing perhaps all the settings required by the play, is made to turn on a vertical shaft which runs down into a concrete anchorage under the center of the circle. It may be made to turn by means of electricity or by hand.

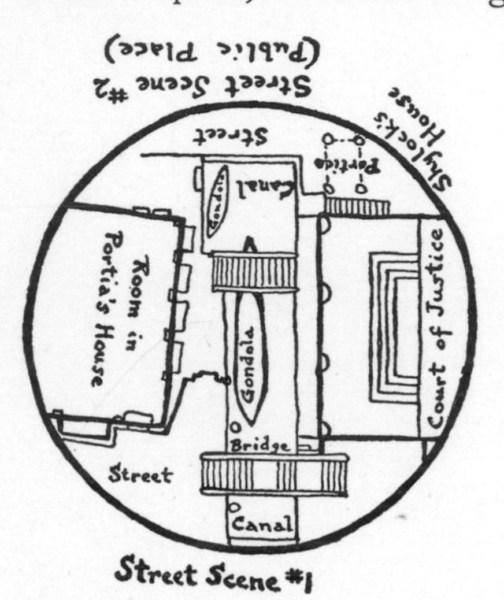


With such a mechanical aid the scene designer need worry no longer over long waits between acts and scenes. The theatres of Germany, where most of the revolving stages have been installed, are enabled thereby to present Shakespeare and other dramatists demanding (if one does not believe in the formal changeless stage) many successive settings during a single performance, with a despatch and a sense of visual continuity unknown elsewhere.

I am taking my diagram of the practical working of the device from that most famous of all examples, Max Reinhardt's *Deutsches Theater* in Berlin. The *drehbühne* is here set for what we may call five major scenes of *The Merchant of Venice*. The extensive Street Scene I probably filled the entire width of the proscenium opening, with a view of a Venetian canal, street, bridge and gondolas. The vista between buildings really runs into the back of Street Scene 2, and the building façades flanking it are moulded on the shells of the two box-set interiors on either side. When the action of the first scene had passed, the stage merely had to be moved a quarter turn to bring the Room in Portia's House before the proscenium opening. Another quarter turn was enough to swing the scene for Act I, Scene 3, a Public Place in Venice, before the audience. The next two scenes are the same in reverse order, thus getting back to the original Street Scene 1. It is probable that the designer and director did not feel it necessary to set separately the Room in Shylock's House (I did not see the production), but played it instead in the scene provided for the later direction "Before Shylock's House." This is cleverly worked into the plan of the five-part setting as one corner of one of the street scenes: a stairway and door that before had been half-hidden became the center of an exterior composition, the street scene glimpsed beyond now having a different aspect on account of the changed angle of sight. The remaining six scenes of this act and four scenes of the next are played in the four settings already revealed, while Act IV, except for the brief street scene at the end, passes in the Court of Justice, which has been set but unused since the beginning. For the rest, there are only two scenes to be provided, the Garden at Belmont and the Avenue to Portia's House, both of which would presumably be set during the one usual long intermission of the evening—if indeed the producers thought it necessary to have these as wholly new backgrounds.

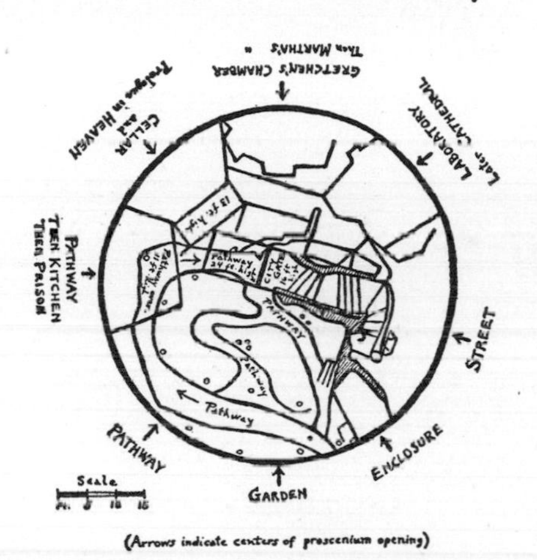


(Arrows indicate centers of proscenium opening)

In short, here is a play demanding, if acted complete, nineteen changes of scene (seven or eight individual settings), a play which in other times was almost universally shortened, mutilated by the re-arranging or telescoping of scenes, and slowed in action by long waits for change of setting—but now presented practically continuously by means of the turn-table stage.

A second diagram shows how the stage was set for the first series of scenes in *Faust* as produced by Reinhardt. Here there are no fewer than eight separate settings that can be brought complete before the audience, on the platform level, and this number is increased to ten by two minor scenes constructed above others, on the two-decker system. Some of the settings also are constructed in such a way that small changes (accomplished easily while action is going on elsewhere) alter them into additional scenes, as the Kitchen of the Sorceress later becomes the Prison, and Marguerite's Chamber is later Martha's Chamber. In this case the demands of the play are for even more widely divergent types of scene and for greater elasticity than in the case of *The Merchant of Venice*, but the problem has been solved adequately and cleverly—and *expeditiously*. I am adding also a sketch by Ernst Stern of the revolving stage as set for the wood scenes of *A Midsummer Night's Dream*. You will remember that the scenes of Acts II and III and the first scene of Act IV are played alternately in "a Wood" and "Another Part of the Wood." What more logical or simple than to set a wood literally (a simplified one, of course) on the turntable, and then to turn another part to the view of the audience as required?

I have thus fully illustrated the capabilities of the revolving stage because I believe that most people not intimately acquainted with its way of working think of it as adequately carrying before the proscenium opening three or four rigidly set single scenes, without visualizing its flexibility and adaptability when capably handled.

The disadvantages of the revolving stage are not to be lightly skipped over, however. Its demands for additional ground space make it too expensive a feature for the American commercial theatre, which is obliged by competition for "trade" to utilize a site in the most costly section of a large city. Moreover, the average speculative American production must be constructed for touring, and no producer in New York dares to design and build his settings in such a manner that they will not serve in any of a half-hundred theatres in New York and a hundred more scattered from coast to coast; and the setting built for a revolving stage is essentially of a special shape and sort, else it has no value. This limitation of the scenery to the one stage for which it is first designed also has retarded the adoption of the invention in England and increasingly throughout Europe. But while expense and considerations of expediency have prevented widespread installation of the device (there are only four full-size turn-table stages in America, I believe, and many of the outstanding European theatres lack them), it is another consideration entirely that seems likely to check further use of the invention. That is the growing conviction that the stage to-day is over-decorated and over-machined, that any sort of scenery that demands such a contraption is a relic of the era of operatic display, that we are all coming inevitably either to a somewhat bare architectural stage or at least to a unit or skeleton sort of setting. But the man who sticks to realism, and wants to present its aspects with a certain degree of visual spread, cannot afford to overlook this ingenious and at times marvelously efficient mechanical servant.

The other very notable advance in the mechanics of scene-shifting is to be witnessed in the development of stage wagons and wagon stages, or sliding stages. While America and the rest of Europe have made experiments in this field, it is again to Germany that one must turn to examine the invention at its best. In many theatres the wagons are just what their name implies: small wheeled vehicles on which various sections of the settings can be fixed, to be rolled into place before the proscenium opening as needed, perhaps three or four or half a dozen being there clamped together to form a complete scene. This is merely an improvement by which large sections of the setting are quickly wheeled into position over the stage floor, instead of small sections being carried or slid by hand, laboriously and one by one.

The invention was further developed, however, through various adaptations of the wagon principle, until the wagon itself became a sliding stage as wide as the proscenium opening. In this case a considerable portion of the old fixed stage floor disappears, and a moving platform carrying a setting slides along tracks parallel to the curtain line into the space before the curtain, to be slid back to its own side at the end of the act, so that a second stage, already set, may move into place from the other side. A variation is a single sliding stage twice as wide as the proscenium opening, so that while one-half is revealed to the audience, the other half is at one side or the other of the proscenium arch and being set with the next background.

The chief drawback to this device is that the whole stage width must be at least three times the width of the proscenium opening, to accommodate the glorified wagon; and besides there must be at the back enough space to store all the settings. Always there is at one side of the proscenium or the other the large floorless space into which the stage will slide—dead space. The

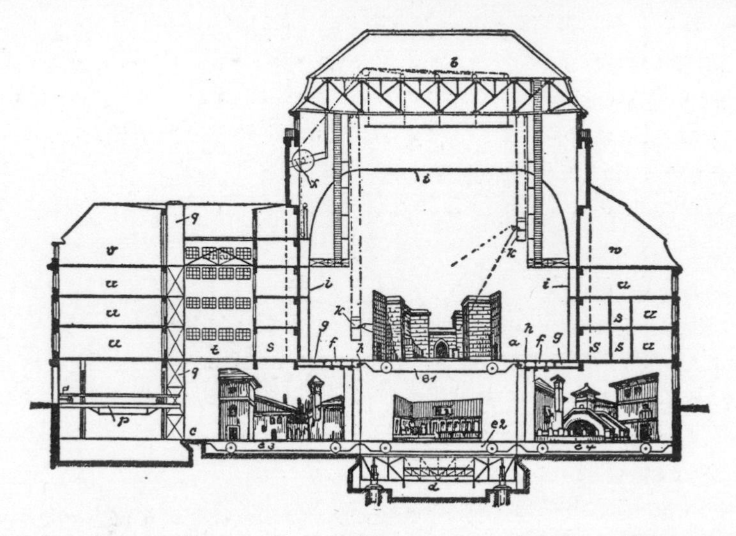

wagon in either its smaller or larger form has a definite advantage over the revolving stage in that there is no reason to cramp the scene, that being the temptation of the designer who wishes to get as many complete settings as possible on to the turn-table.

An extraordinary example of the sliding stage is to be found in the Dresden State Theatre. Space was not available for installation of the device on the stage level, so that the immense "wagon" or acting floor bearing the complete setting (really a section of the stage floor as wide as the proscenium, with wheels fixed on the under framework) is lowered like a huge elevator to a cellar under the theatre before being slid to one side or the other. A second stage is then wheeled to the central position and elevated to the stage-floor level. As a matter of fact there are two sections in each of the two immense stage-wagons, so that if desired only one half of the setting need be lowered and slid off. This breaking of the stage wagon (on a line parallel with the curtain) also allows variations of acting levels, since the two sections may be elevated to different heights; and behind the space into which the double wagon-stage rises is a section which is on an elevator but without the wagon feature.

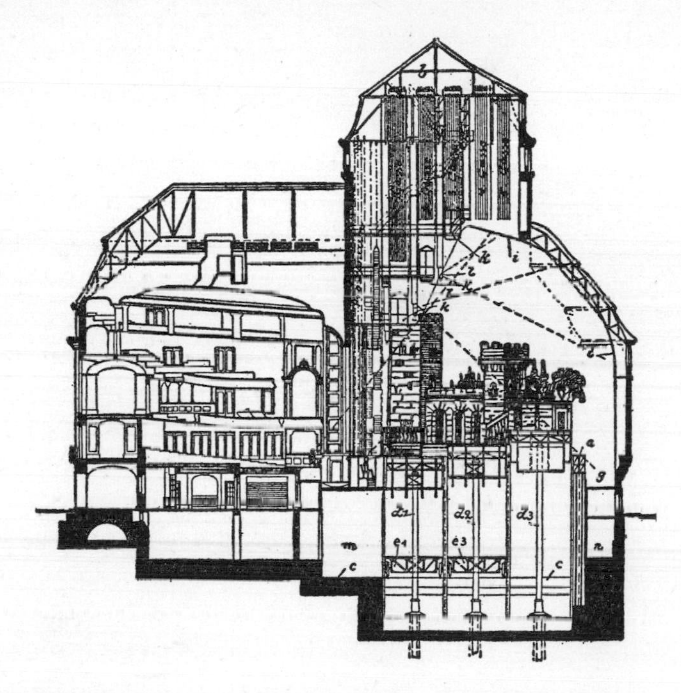

Certain details of this stage can be understood best by a study of the explanatory cross section shown on page 60. The upper setting is shown in the stage space as seen by the audience. This setting rests on a wheeled wagon, seen below the stage floor level; and reference to the longitudinal section on this page will show that the wagon in turn is on a platform which can be lifted or sunk by hydraulic elevators. When the wagon E1 is lowered, it comes into the position occupied in the first diagram by wagon E2. From here it is wheeled by electricity into the position E3 or E4, whichever is unoccupied. It is clear that small stage wagons carrying sections of the setting can still be used to expedite the assembling of scenery on the larger wagon-stage, as on a fixed stage.

The longitudinal section indicates how large in such a theatre is the space dedicated to stage and stage machinery as compared with the audience space. This diagram also indicates the relationship of the setting, as built on the double wagon-stage and the elevator stage behind, to the cupola-horizon or stage dome.

A true cupola-horizon, in its theoretically perfect form, is a stage background in the shape of a half-dome curving around the playing stage at the sides and up over the stage from the back forward toward the proscenium wall. Its surface is such that under proper lighting it affords the spectator a sense of merely looking into a cushion of air, or into a cloudless sky. Its advantage over any other form of background behind the setting is that it is perfectly natural (once a powerful recommendation in itself) and at the same time wholly unobtrusive. It also permits delicacy and subtlety of lighting unknown before its introduction.

Back in the days of painted landscape backdrops, the sky was a minor element even in the design of outdoor scenes, unless the artist chose to spread himself on cloud effects. But as landscape drops went out of fashion, in favor of naturalistic set scenes, the cyclorama drop, a curtain usually painted in flat light blue, came into use, and was a mighty improvement. When well stretched, without wrinkles, and cunningly lighted, it afforded a neutral background, giving the illusion of distance without drawing the eye from the foreground, and often achieving atmospheric effects that were a distinct aid to the drama. It would wrinkle at times, however, and it would shiver in the breeze when someone opened the stage door. Moreover, it often could not be hung in such fashion that the old borders or sky-cloths could be done away with; it was not high enough to complete the vista at the top.

I think it was Fortuny who first developed the dome idea, in connection with the lighting system that bears his name. The material of his half-dome was silk stretched tight, because he had discovered that he could obtain a special quality of light by reflecting it from silk. But later experiment proved the value of plaster as a reflecting surface, and practically all the more recent developments of the horizon-dome have utilized plaster as material. The texture is such that light reflected from it has a beautiful effect of liveliness without any sheen or any tangible objective interest. The diffused light thus obtained is "atmospheric" in the best sense. The background is inconspicuously luminous without being noticeably illuminated. It is a perfect servant to both the realist seeking naturalness and the artist working with suggestive or abstract elements.

By its slope forward at the top, over part of the stage setting, the dome affords the same cushion to the spectator's eye above as at the back, doing away with the necessity for cloth borders. The longitudinal section of the Dresden State Theatre shows the curve of the *horizont* over a large portion of the stage area, and illustrates graphically how a spectator in the first rows of seats may look upward as far as the proscenium arch will permit and see only the neutral plaster surface. The dome here thrusts forward at each side only to the front line of the rearmost of the elevator stages. A dome on a base describing a full half-circle is usually considered to blanket too much of the stage space, unduly hindering the process of setting, and it is manifestly impossible with a sliding stage. Therefore in most examples the curve is flattened, retaining enough of the thrust forward at each end to present the plaster surface to the spectator's view from what may be considered every *reasonable* standpoint. In some theatres with revolving stages the complete half-dome has been built, and at the *Volksbühne* in Berlin the ends are extended forward on tangents beyond the half-circle.

Critics of the dome cite as disadvantages the blanketing of much of the old flying space, the preventing of direct access to a considerable part of the stage, and costliness. These objections have combined to prevent anything like universal adoption of the feature; although it is a poor theatre in Germany that has not some sort of *horizont*. In America it has remained for the little and non-commercial theatres to prove the resources for beauty that are in the invention, as the tiny Provincetown Playhouse in New York has done, and the Goodman Memorial Theatre in Chicago; and less perfectly, the Neighborhood Playhouse in New York and the Arts and Crafts Playhouse in Detroit, with plaster wall backgrounds only slightly curved toward the dome shape. Recently there was invented in Germany a new sort of cloth cyclorama which can be unrolled and carried around the stage on curved tracks, which is said to give as fine diffusion and quality of light as plaster. It is being exploited, together with a special lighting equipment, under the name "Ars System," and it promises a new efficiency in combined simplicity and capability for beauty.

The dome or plaster wall (or perfected cyclorama) made possible what is called "projected scenery." Here an image is thrown on the neutral background with an instrument not unlike the old-fashioned "magic lantern," but with all the advantage of modern improvements in quality of light, color richness and creative composition. The designer makes merely a miniature sketch or negative of the scene, and this is projected on the "screen" and serves as an impressionistic background for the action. I do not wish to go into detail here regarding the methods by which the image is made normal when straight-front projection is impossible, or other technical points; for in spite of the admirable simplicity of the device, and a beautiful clarity of scene occasionally achieved, it is not in the direct line of modern progress—perhaps merely a way of bringing the painter less offensively into the theatre. The projected picture is likely to be disturbingly pictorial and thus out of harmony with the actuality of the actor. I think that our lighting experts gained something out of the projecting machine, for greater flexibility in abstract and expressive lighting. Along a parallel line, as a by-product of the invention of his color organ, the instrument by which he has all but completed creation of a new art, "mobile color," Thomas Wilfred has developed machines for projecting either pictorial settings or colored light, and has achieved tonal qualities beyond what stage designers had dreamed possible.

The use of projected scenery in America has been limited, and Lee Simonson has been most successful of the experimenters, in his work for the Theatre Guild. In Europe the Germans, who perfected the method, obtained interesting, and at the time advanced, results, but seem now to have set aside the projecting machine except as a minor auxiliary mechanism.

I have several times mentioned incidentally the great progress made in developing more flexible and more sensitive lighting equipment. Only a detailed handbook could tell of the successive technical changes during the last thirty years, and explain the mechanism by which the extraordinarily expressive stage light of to-day is obtained. The increasing tendency to let light do the work of "scenery," however, makes the subject in its broader aspects necessarily a part of any essay on stage decoration.

In the first place it will be noticed that dependence upon light is directly in line with the aims of the successive artists who have so changed the practice of stage setting. To the naturalists the invention of "truer" lighting, in place of the old white glare, made it possible to illumine a scene more naturally. Indeed, the arch-naturalist Belasco was the pioneer in America in discovering methods which would eliminate footlights and the sort of distortion they caused, and border lights that falsely over-emphasized the edges of the stage picture.

Then on the long trail of simplification, there was no other medium quite so responsive as light. The beauty of light, even of richly colored and varied light, is above all a simple beauty. And unity and continuity of lighting beauty might almost convince one that there was unity in the play and acting. If the picture must be made atmospheric, not literal, light was the magic for that. As in painting, only a deeper study of light, a finer mastery, could bring the appealing, if frail, loveliness of Impressionism. While a pillar and a candelabra cunningly placed might correctly suggest the whole cathedral in *Faust*, it was lighting that carried the deeper spiritual intimation, the emotion of the place. Suggestion, emotional intimation, dramatic presence, mood—they all reside in this thing that consciously or sub-consciously we all react to almost as did those deifiers of light, the Sun-worshipers. Certainly there is no other God before this one in the scenic studios of the modern theatre.

As candles gave way to oil in the footlights, oil to gas, gas to electricity, the gain was in the quantity of light rather than the quality. Indeed, gas gave a softer, sweeter light than the first developments of electricity. But once enough intensity had been gained—and for years it was far too much—the artists turned their attention to widening the range of manipulation, to gaining a control which would allow them to have a little or a great deal, and to spread it or spot it. The naturalists, as a matter of fact, not only achieved excellent control, but took much of the unnecessary glare out of illumination—substituting light as true to life as the nose on your face.

Flexibility was gained in many ways. First the individual electric bulbs, originally yellowish in tone and therefore bringing out certain colors falsely, were carried through a series of improvements until the present white bulb emerged, in a range of sizes from the smallest up to the 1500-watt lamp.* Instead of rows of small bulbs placed almost exclusively in the footlight trough and along the borders, the lighting "units" became bewilderingly diversified. Portable lamps, bunches and strips, for flood or spot purposes, were added to border lights for general illumination, and the sources of light spread from footlight trough and borders to every conceivable hidden position on the stage, and even into hidden boxes before the curtain line—in a bulge above the proscenium front, under the balcony railing, in the paneling of the auditorium ceiling. The strips became not long rigid rows of small bulbs, but articulated groups of half a dozen high-powered lamps, each capable of turning individually on the strip axis and each fitted with full color range. The projection machines, too, offer the widest range of types, and extraordinary adaptability in each machine. The focusing spotlight of a few years back now resides in a hood and behind a lens that makes it a flood light or spot at will, for short or long range. Terms like "soft edge spot" are in themselves suggestive of the delicate shades of lighting practice. Single dimmers and banks of dimmers make it possible to bring up or lower the lights singly, in groups or as one battery, instead of switching them on or off, or jumping them. Color is no longer a matter of using colored bulbs; instead, there are mediums of the right colors on the lamp boxes, to be slid into place instantly as required: color filters of glass or gelatine.

If all these changes seem to be in the mechanics of lighting, it is nevertheless the quality of illumination that has changed most. Ten years ago, when we had just begun to get out of the glare period, and the simplest orchestration of light seemed almost a miracle, an Italian named Fortuny developed for German theatres a lighting system flexible beyond all previous dreams, and particularly notable for the quality of the light obtained. For

* The 3000-watt lamp has been developed for exceptional use, and one even hears rumors of a 5000-watt bulb.

several years every progressive theatre wanted a Fortuny system, which was in effect a method of throwing light away from the stage scene to have it reflected back from silken surfaces that added color and luminosity and liveliness to the rays—and diffused them. It is typical of later progress that within a few years other theatre artists developed inventions that obtain the same lovely quality of light in direct illumination, without the extra step of a reflector.

Footlights, illuminating the under portions of the actor's nose and chin, but obscuring in shadow the more expressive portions of his face, were soon suppressed, and in cases abolished. But to-day they have come back to a reasonable use, as one instrument in a considerable orchestra—for all artistic lighting cannot take Rembrandt as an inspiration, with dramatic floods of light played against deep shadows.

Beyond these general observations on the advance in lighting I do not feel it necessary to go. There are methods of lighting semi-transparent curtains or gauzes from behind to produce special effects, and methods of painting scenery so that it carries two separate pictures, one becoming apparent to the audience under one color of light, only to disappear when a different colored lamp literally "brings to light" the other picture.

This same principle applies in that technical method of painting the flats called *pointillisme.* Little points of different colored paints are daubed on to the canvas in juxtaposition, in such a way that under blue lighting only the blue in the surface definitely comes to life, under red light only red, and so on. Beyond the possibility of bringing out or killing certain colors in the surface, the method brings the advantages which the Impressionists, Pointillists and Divisionists gained in easel painting: freshness of color, an atmospheric liveliness, vibration of light. The system has so many advantages over the old flat and generally muddy painting, that when it was first introduced to the American stage by Joseph Urban a dozen years ago, it was hailed as in itself a revolution of considerable moment. The other progressive designers incorporated it into their practice, and they still call upon its potentialities freely. Gradually, if more tardily, the commercial scenic studios adopted it, for better or for worse, where it belonged and where its liveliness was out of place. In some form or other, indeed, "broken color" is almost the universal rule, and in general the change is very much for the better.

One other mechanical or physical change on the stage of the twentieth-century theatre deserves brief description, although its importance is as a symptom of a greater change coming, rather than as an immediate aid to realistic drama. It is the construction of temporary "portals" at the front of the stage picture, and the building of various sorts of skeleton settings on which varied scenes are constructed by changes of minor elements.

The portals, doorways standing throughout a performance, and used arbitrarily for entries and exits with either indoor or outdoor settings, are a revival of a feature of the Restoration theatres, where the proscenium frame was pierced by two permanent doorways giving access to the forestage or apron. In the current theatre they may be built into a false outer proscenium before the curtain line, if the stage has enough apron space, or into an inner proscenium inside the curtain line. In the latter case a second curtain is usually hung just back of the false proscenium and portals, providing an outer and an inner stage, and thus making possible more expeditious running through of the scenes.

Revival of the device is traceable to the experiments made by the Germans in an effort to find an adequate stage for the production of Shakespeare. As early as 1840, indeed, Immermann's "Shakespeare Stage" at Dusseldorf showed this feature, and there are recurrences down to the early years of the current century. Some of us consider this an intermediate step between the proscenium-frame stage and a coming wholly formal, non-pictorial stage.

Joseph Urban was probably the first to utilize the specially built portals in America. Robert Edmond Jones, Rollo Peters, Norman-Bel Geddes and Lee Simonson have used them freely at times, always (it seems to me) with a gain in the theatrical and dramatic values. The advantage is not only in the elimination of disillusioning waits between scenes, but in the audience's sense of being always in the theatre, at the same theatre—as against the old system where the scenic designer spent his talent trying to give the spectator an illusion of being away from a stage and in a succession of real places. (A difficult distinction, but at the very heart of modernist theories of the theatre.) The standing portals also afford a sub-conscious feeling of holding together the action, of continuity, of oneness, a sort of continuous physical accompaniment that has its tying-together effect like the accompaniment of appropriate light or music.

In the last analysis, this is a method of formalizing or conventionalizing the front portion of the stage, while keeping the up-stage space free for more or less realistic manipulation.

The value of the skeleton setting likewise lies in the double service of making possible more rapid changes and carrying through a visual sense of oneness. In some cases an actual framework is constructed to remain throughout the play. I am adding here a thumbnail sketch by Sheldon K. Viele for the New York Theatre Guild's production of *The Cloister*, where an arcade with three arches permanently separated the front of the stage from an inner scene. Other examples of the device are illustrated in the photographs of *Malvaloca* as produced by the Actors' Theatre and *The Love of the Three Oranges* as produced by the Chicago Opera Company. Claude Bragdon's designs for *Hamlet* follow the same system with somewhat more abstract elements.

When this process of simplification and conventionalization is carried a little farther, we step out of the realistic-representative field altogether, and come to the abstract multiple settings that can be used interchangeably for any but the most literal slice-of-life plays. But they belong to a theory of production which will be discussed when we get nearer to the truly formal stages.

In writing of the period beginning with the naturalistic revolt and extending through the efforts of the most talented "practical" decorators to mount the current drama with becoming simplicity, unity and harmony, to surround it with an alluring atmosphere and to render its action mechanically fluent, I have set up several signposts indicating an approach toward the subject of formal stages and abstract settings. In all that I have described so far, the setting has been conceived primarily *as a picture*, despite the passing of the painter of perspective, and despite the placing of plastic objects and the use of flat walls in the picture. Always, too, the artists have been seeking reality of place, putting emphasis on the elements that indicated the locale of the action. However much they simplified, made suggestive, and stylized, they were working with a realistic intent. What they simplified was real rooms, gardens or forests, what they suggested was actuality, what they stylized was a succession of places outside the theatre. The painter, having learned the inadequacy of easel-painting in the theatre, was trying other means than painting—but as yet he was not utilizing primarily *the theatre*.

Although I have thus treated together all this matter of bringing the current realistic stage to a pleasant prettiness, in time it was everywhere paralleled by experiments with formal stages, with abstract multiple settings, with anti-realistic devices such as screens and curtains. I have left these for later description because I wanted to emphasize the dividing line between the two currents of effort. When Craig and Appia gave expression to their ideas about simplification and conventionalization, about using essentially theatric materials instead of those borrowed from other arts, the current stage was simply crying aloud for revolution and reform. It was already decades behind the other arts in feeling any breath of the modern spirit. The greater number of those who heeded the cry of the two leaders, wanted more than anything else to make the new ideas "practical." They were confused in mind because they saw before them no theatres in which Craig's ideas could be realized *in toto* immediately. The stage before them was a peep-hole realistic stage. They descended upon it and compromised to meet its conditions. We have seen how remarkably they dressed it, bettered it, largely through those very principles that Craig and Appia had set forth—excepting that one central, essential, deeply revolutionary precept that the Western world must get back to the stage as stage, the theatre as theatre.

Here then is the dividing line between the two larger parts of my book.

In treating twentieth-century stage decoration, one-half—enormously more than one-half in actual practice—is seen to fit contentedly into the old proscenium-frame theatre, not without extraordinary improvements; the other half demands, and experiments with, new forms of stage.

# VII

## VISIONS OF A DIFFERENT THEATRE: CRAIG AND APPIA

IT would be idle to think that Gordon Craig single-handed, out of his own thoughts and love alone, accomplished a revolution. He was rather the figure in which the growing forces of revolt against a tyrannical past came together, the prophet who directed a thousand artists toward a different future. Clear reason and the power of visionary and visual design are combined among his attributes in a rare degree. He both saw understandingly and could express himself vigorously, on the stage, in writing, in black-and-white design.

There were others before him, however, who guessed the emptiness of the current theatre, and particularly the triviality and falsity of stage decoration when measured by any art standard. Thus Schlegel a full hundred years earlier wrote: "Our system of decoration was properly invented for the opera, to which in reality it is also best adapted. . . . Among the inevitable defects, I reckon the breaking of the lines in the side scenes from every point of view except one; the disproportion of the player when he appears in the background against objects diminished in perspective; the unfavorable lighting from below and behind; the contrast between the painted and the actual lights and shades; the impossibility of narrowing the stage at pleasure, so that the inside of a palace and a hut have the same length and breadth. The errors which may be avoided are want of simplicity and of great and reposeful masses; the overloading of the scene with superfluous and distracting objects . . .; an architecture full of mannerism, often altogether unconnected, nay, even at variance with, possibility . . ."

Wagner in his time made protest against the lack of unity in the theatre and accomplished a sort of reform of the scene, and from Immermann in mid-century to Savits in the 'nineties there were other sporadic attacks and experiments in Germany. Craig's own father, the architect E. W. Godwin, was among those few in England who foresaw great changes in theatre art and in setting; and in France one finds de Fouquières writing in 1884 on *l'Art de la Mise en Scène,* and very skeptical about the form of the current theatre and the current methods of staging, although he offered no radical suggestions for a solution. The larger theatre, indeed, remained untouched by any real wave of combined protest and constructive thought until Appia and Craig came forward with their books, designs and rare productions in the few years on either side of 1900.

I would like to quote a passage from a book of one of these men and say, "here is the starting point of the new movement in the theatre." But they did not express themselves clearly and completely all at once. Their ideas grew as they wrote and worked and made designs—although on one point they both became clear and explicit very early: the contemporary theatre was becoming a slave to the realists, its art lacked unity, and contemporary staging was generally false and inadequate.

Nothing but a considerable patchwork of sentences and paragraphs, a weaving together of cryptic hints, sudden illuminating phrases and vague intimations, can afford the sense of Craig's vision, and chart even roughly the drift of his ideas. But almost any quotation will indicate why he irritated some readers, and provoked others into revolt, why he is invariably recognized as the great *stimulating* force behind modernist effort.

One can begin best, perhaps, by quoting again that most-quoted passage in which Craig pointed out the lack of true masters of the art of the theatre:*

"I have many times written that there is only one way to obtain unity in the Art of the Theatre. I suppose it is unnecessary to explain why unity should be there as in other great arts; I suppose that it offends no one to admit that unless unity reigns 'chaos is come again.' . . . Let me make a list (an incomplete one, but it will serve) of the different workers in the theatre. When I have made this list I will tell you how many are head-cooks and how they assist in the spoiling of the broth. . . . [He then lists the workers, from the proprietor, business manager and stage director through the actors and actresses, the designer of settings, the designer of costumes, the stage crew, etc., etc.]

* This quotation and those following, except where specially noted, are from Craig's *On the Art of the Theatre,* London, 1911, and Chicago, 1911; this book being an expansion of a brochure entitled *The Art of the Theatre,* first published in 1905.

"Now look carefully at this list. We see seven heads and two very influential members. Seven directors instead of one, and nine opinions instead of one.

"*Now, then, it is impossible for a work of art ever to be produced where more than one brain is permitted to direct; and if works of art are not seen in the theatre this one reason is a sufficient one, though there are plenty more.*

"Do you wish to know why there are seven masters instead of one? It is because there is no one man in the theatre who is a master in himself, that is to say, there is no one man capable of inventing and rehearsing a play: capable of designing and superintending the construction of both scenery and costume: of writing any necessary music: of inventing such machinery as is needed and the lighting that is to be used."

It is this statement more than any other one thing that has brought into the theatre during the last twenty years that all-powerful, all-seeing artist-director: the regisseur who either is himself designer of the stage background or imparts to a fellow-artist his conception of the staging and directs the execution of every detail. With Craig, of course, there is no question of the regisseur and designer being other than one and the same creative artist, but in practice there are not half a dozen men living who combine even near-mastery in both fields. The idea has worked out in such manner, however, that the theatre to-day, whatever its persisting imperfections, is organized incomparably better than twenty years ago, for artistic control, for coördinate creation in the several departments of staging under unified direction. At any rate, stage decoration is no longer something ordered in without supervision from an unrelated scenic studio.

It is noteworthy that in the passage quoted above, as in so much of Craig's writing, there is that insistence on a *complete* art, that stressing of coördinate mastery, which must underlie any permanent betterment. Craig so many times has been blindly accused of wanting to substitute decoration for drama that it is wise to emphasize this completeness of conception. Elsewhere, although he may be as roundabout, as cryptic as ever about the attributes and methods of the art, he leaves no doubt about this fundamental point:

"The art of the theatre is neither acting nor the play, it is not scene nor dance, but it consists of all the elements of which these things are composed: action, which is the very spirit of acting; words, which are the body of the play; line and color, which are the very heart of the scene; rhythm, which is the very essence of dance. One is no more important than the other, no more than one color is more important to a painter than another, or one note more important than another to a musician."

The conception of a different theatre, however, is shadowed forth best from those writings that deal with realism on the stage—that arraign it scathingly at times—and with the interpretation of the word "action." Craig insists upon the importance of action as *movement*—not merely action in the story-development sense. He wants *visual beauty* to characterize the production throughout, not in the painter's way, but by every means that is typically and essentially theatrical. He goes back to the definition and derivation of the word "theatre" to prove that the theatre is first of all a place for *seeing*. In a footnote on the first page of a book of his designs, called *Towards a New Theatre*, he puts this definition, with its pungent afterthought:

"THEATRE.—According to Professor Skeat, a French word . . . Derived from the Latin *theatrum*, derived from the Greek Θέατρον, a place for seeing shows, derived from the Greek Θεαομαι, I see. . . .

"Note: Not a word about it being a place for hearing 30,000 words babbled out in two hours."

In opposition to the theory of realistic illusion he put down this notably true observation:* "In what we call Decoration of our theatre . . . there would be no attempt to produce what we call 'theatrical illusion.' For instance, we should not paint a tree, or put up an imitation tree so as best to copy in color and texture a real tree. No more than in a cathedral they put up a wooden copy of the original cross. Doubtless the cross on which the Saviour was crucified was an ordinary and rough wooden structure, but when it reaches the cathedral it becomes a precious work of art, in no way realistic."

It remained for others to elaborate, perhaps to make clear, Craig's vision of a different theatre. At least a whole theory has crystallized around the

* *The Theatre Advancing*. London and Boston, 1919.

idea that seems to be at the heart of his writings: that the art of the theatre, beyond having that unity which is an attribute of all art, and utilizing to the full the values of that action which is its own essential feature, will abandon the ideal of an illusion of reality, the ideal of faithful if selective representation of something happening naturally; will instead present a show that is typically and recognizably theatrical. Certain writers have called it a *Presentative* type of production, as against the representative that imitates nature, that is based primarily on observation and transcribes photographically. The theory is based on the idea that there is a theatrical "form," some quality above and enveloping the materials of the art, movement, voice, scene, which can be revealed in the manipulation of the production—something as intangible and vital as the "significant form" in painting or essentially sculptural or architectural form. When this essentially theatric emotion, growing out of the masterly use of all the resources of the stage, grips the spectator, he is not merely looking at a clever or amusing or affecting imitation of some real characters and real incidents, but is instead on a plane with the gods, where life is intensified, epitomized, clarified. He is not led to believe that he is partaking of life as lived, but is conscious that he is above life, in a theatre, in a region of theatric imagination. The stage is not disguised, lost in a picture. It is frankly and formally a platform for acting—and the spectator accepts the convention, dismisses the commonplacenesses of life, and prepares his mind and emotions for the nobility of the theatre.

Craig, as I say, never so definitely tried to pin down his vision of a new art, and he probably would scoff at such terms as "presentative" and "purely formal." He has hidden his ideal behind half-statements and intimations; but in the larger view, he started a ball rolling, and as it has gathered momentum through the years it has clearly and unmistakably turned down the alley of these people who talk about the presentative stage. And to understand either Craig's work or the development of stage decoration from here on, you must have a conception of theatre form as such, of the naked stage as distinguished from stage pictures, of enjoyment of art within the convention set up by the artist as against enjoyment of an illusion of reality.

In a chapter in which he outlined his method of conceiving and putting down the designs for a production of *Macbeth,* Craig foreshadowed every one of those ideas which gave us the catchwords mentioned some pages back: unity, simplicity, suggestion, design and the rest. The following quotations are typical of the fullness of his vision:

". . . It is the large and sweeping impression produced by means of scene and the movement of the figures, which is undoubtedly the most valuable means at your disposal. . . . It is idle to talk about the distraction of scenery, because the question here is not how to create some distracting scenery, but rather how to create a place which harmonizes with the thoughts of the poet. . . . Remember that on a sheet of paper which is but two inches square you can make a line which seems to tower miles in the air, and you can do the same on your stage, for it is all a matter of proportion and nothing to do with actuality. . . .

"Your success will depend upon your capacity to make variations upon these two themes; but remember never to let go of the main theme of the play when searching for variations in the scene. By means of your scene you will be able to mould the movements of the actors, and you must be able to increase the impression of your numbers without actually adding another man to your forty or fifty. You must not, therefore, waste a single man, nor place him in such a position that an inch of him is lost. Therefore the place on which he walks must be the most carefully studied part of the whole scene. But in telling you not to waste an inch of him I do not therefore mean to convey that you must *show* every inch of him. It is needless to say more on this point. By means of suggestion you may bring on the stage a sense of all things—the rain, the sun, the wind, the snow, the hail, the intense heat—but you will never bring them there by attempting to wrestle and close with Nature, in order so that you may seize some of her treasure and lay it before the eyes of the multitude. By means of suggestion in movement you may translate all the passions and the thoughts of vast numbers of people, or by means of the same you can assist your actor to convey the thoughts and the emotions of the particular character he impersonates. Actuality, accuracy of detail, is useless upon the stage. . . .

"I let my scenes grow out of not merely the play, but from broad sweeps of thought which the play has conjured up in me. . . . We are concerned with the heart of this thing, and with loving and understanding it. Therefore approach it from all sides, surround it, and do not let yourself be attracted away by the idea of scene as an end in itself, of costume as an end in itself, or of stage management or any of these things, and never lose hold of your determination to win through to the secret—the secret which lies in the creation of another beauty. . . ."

Craig's designs are so clearly examples of his non-realistic, coöperative, thoughtful attitude, and are so expressive, that I need say little further in regard to the seven which are included among my plates. They indicate both the way in which he reached forward to abstract means, and his reliance upon the values of light. The reader should be reminded that when they were first exhibited and published, in many parts of Europe, they were so absolutely revolutionary, so unlike anything on the stages of the time, that the theatre world found it difficult to take them seriously. They came, of course, long before those examples of simplified and stylized realism which precede them in this book. At that time Adolphe Appia alone had been daring and far seeing enough to design works comparable to these.

Appia's earlier contribution was less to the larger questions of new playhouses, new dramas and a different conception of the art of the theatre; it more particularly concerned the scene and the actor's place in it. He wrote even before Craig of the inadequacy and falsity of the flat painted setting and the methods employed to light it, and of the futility of realism; and he also pointed out the values that might be gained through an artist's manipulation of the actor's movements. But chiefly it was in his vision of the possibilities of light as an expressive medium that he foreshadowed a great part of twentieth-century progress in stagecraft. His books were too erudite and involved for wide circulation, and too seldom achieved translation from language to language; but his beautifully rendered drawings were more widely reproduced, and are continuing after thirty years to instruct by example.

In the first place Appia went back to that foundation principle—revolutionary in 1899—that there must be unity of play, scene and action. The current scene, he noted, made such unity impossible. The setting was made up of inanimate objects and materials; and the two-dimensional art of the painter, in a tortured form, was wrongly introduced into what should be a place of three-dimensional space and light. The scene was dead while the actor was living.

"In the theatre," he wrote,* "we are present at a dramatic *action;* it is the presence of the player in the scene that gives rise to this action; without the players there is no action." Again he wrote that the actor is "the one essential of the *mise-en-scène;* it is he that we come to see, it is to him that we look for the emotion, and it is this emotion that we have come here to seek. Our business then is above all else to lay the foundation of the *mise-en-scène* in the actuality of the actor, and therefore to clear it of everything that is out of keeping with his presence."

Determining that the painter should therefore no longer determine the conditions of the *mise-en-scène,* that a mode of setting should be developed that would emphasize the actor above all, that the surroundings must be "living" and three-dimensional, Appia turned to light as a medium. The current setting was lighted practically flat, like a picture. But Appia foresaw that the elements necessary to the background could be subordinated, and living light be made to fill the stage, or a living play of light and shadow. Be it noted that the mechanical means to this sort of stage lighting were nowhere available, had not been invented. In his thought and in his designs he had jumped twenty years ahead of the progress of the world.

Appia did not quickly grasp at abstraction as Craig did. He did not make use of line, proportion, architectural mass, so freely, for he was not thinking in terms of an entirely different stage, in those early years. He contented himself with giving atmosphere and depth to the stage, minimizing the physical setting as far as then seemed practical, and softening, veiling, dramatizing it with light. He succeeded in making his stage primarily sculptural rather than pictorial—grasping the principle of "the plastic" almost a generation before it came to common acceptance—and thus brought to an end the conflict between the actor and the scene.

He used light both as a dramatic medium in itself and as a unifying force, binding actor and setting together, and harmonizing both with the music—for all his early work was done with reference to Wagnerian drama.

* Adolphe Appia: *Die Musik und die Inscenierung.* Munich, 1899.

In his drawings, seldom if ever made to indicate a single setting, but always in series showing the changing lighting in relation to the action and the spiritual progression of the play, he designed the gradations, the composition and the projection of the lighting down to the smallest detail. He knew just where the face of a given character would come into full illumination, and just when a figure would creep into silhouette before just such a quality of light. He not only followed the emotion of the play, but heightened it, by manipulating the masses of light and shadow, majestically or restfully, by playing the action against bursts of light or veils of darkness, by fogging one scene mysteriously and making the next glorious with light.

"We shall seek no longer," he wrote, "to afford the illusion of a forest, but only the illusion of a man in the atmosphere of a forest. . . . And when the trees, lightly stirred by the breeze, attract the attention of Siegfried, the spectators should see Siegfried bathed in light and living shadows, and not some stage 'cut-outs' arbitrarily set in movement."

Again he commented on the antagonism between paint and light: light may be used to make visible a vertical canvas, but that has nothing to do with the rôle of light in its own creative field. "Light is in itself an element of unlimited potentialities; used freely, it is for us of the theatre what the palette is to the painter; every combination of color is possible to it."

Later, Appia in his experiments and in new series of drawings abandoned entirely what he had taken from the old stage picture, and experimented with architectural masses and steps until he developed a new sort of formal stage. The actor's presence remained his one starting point, but he found a new importance in movement and space. The later phase of his work only within a very few years has come to the attention of the world; and important as it is proving to be, "light" is the word by which his service to the modern theatre is likely to be perpetually recognized. The scene made to live in light, light as a binding force, dramatic light, dynamic light, light the perfect slave, unifying, clarifying, emotionalizing, light deified.

The artists who are generally credited with developing the new stagecraft practically, the leaders after Craig and Appia, really had this whole story before them when they began. If they had understood and believed in these two pioneers beyond the desire to compromise, if they had dared to turn away from the realistic theatre, some one of them might have accomplished undiluted what the pioneers dreamed. What these others have gained is good enough, perhaps, in a too commonplace world; but let us remember that it was Appia and Craig whose ideas were adapted and compromised, to improve a thing that interested them not at all—but that seemed to most men worth saving. And let us remember that Craig and Appia are still the outstanding geniuses among the later radicals, are still working shoulder to shoulder with all those who are reaching out uncompromisingly toward the true new stage. Nor is there any leader, any basic theorist, to place beside them. In treating their work thus at length, I have sketched the theories that underlie all the accomplishments with which the rest of this book will be concerned.

Of course the dividing line between the compromise realistic stage and the manifestations of the new theory is none too clear. Some things in the first half of my book might justly be put in the latter half, and some yet to be talked about may have earthly rags about them which should put them back with the hosts of the prettified realistic. But in general I shall treat from here on matters related to the search for a new stage and a new drama, the effort for typically theatrical expressiveness, the reach toward the beauties that lie close to abstraction and revealed form.

# VIII

## THE REACH TOWARD ABSTRACT MEANS

EVEN with Craig and Appia, as we have seen, there was no immediate formulation of the details of a typically theatric stage. Appia even admitted into his newly plastic scene such traces of the old scene-painter's technique as the painted "cut-out" branches of trees, while Craig went through periods of designing with differing abstract elements such as curtains, towering architectural masses, and finally screens. These were important as steps, being outside the realistic intent, but they were usually experiments in one part of staging—where perhaps a stage itself was needed. After the development of a theory of the abstract, these were thrusts toward creation of concrete means.

Curtains particularly have held a fascination for the progressive designer. I speak not of the old-time proscenium curtain or of the drop curtain, stretched tight, and as likely as not painted with a scene, but rather of curtains as sheer fabrics hanging in folds. These have taken a large place on the formal stages of other times: for instance, on the platforms from which the scholastic plays were acted, and the English Elizabethan stage. For the modern decorator the impulse toward them came partly from the renaissance of interest in the old non-pictorial acting platforms, and partly from actual experiment based on the theory of "the less setting the better"—experiment toward *any* background that would leave the actor free, outstanding, and unhampered master of the stage.

The values of curtains either as full background or as a unit are obvious, if one has decided to abandon the realistic formula. They are only as positive as the designer wishes to make them: disappearing into a neutrality and colorless retirement if that is fitting, or coming forward to serve decoratively with color, all over pattern or even an ornamental device, if such contributive expressiveness is in keeping with the spirit of the play and action. The range of beauty and texture is almost unlimited, granted that one has made a study of fabrics and colors under lighting, and there is great abstract value in the arrangement of the folds and major masses.

As a medium they fit in with most of the theories of non-representative staging: they leave the imagination of the spectator free, they form an unobtrusive background that shows forth the actor emphasized, they are plastic, they take light effectively and sensitively, as commonly hung they are contributive in their natural rhythmic value. In short, they offer a simple, harmonious means to abstract decorativeness.

As used, they have varied from box-like or semi-circular arrangements of sheer and plain hangings, to sensuously colored and elaborately lighted piles of fabric. On Fuchs' "relief stage" they were frankly flat backgrounds for acting figures, and no more; on Reinhardt's stage they took on expressive color and exotic pattern; with Granville-Barker and Norman Wilkinson they carried pictorial scenes decoratively treated, with the folds belying any realistic intention; with Bakst they were additional means to pile up color gorgeously, to swell in appealing sensuous line, to complete a painter's realization of a voluptuous Oriental love-nest.

Gordon Craig utilized curtains in his early designs and productions, but I think usually in connection with architectural constructions. His later work almost eliminates them, in favor of more stable, solid and rigid architectural pylons and screens. Indeed, it seems that most of the outstanding modern designers have gone through a period of utilizing hangings as a mainstay, later to find greater potentialities in harder and less effeminate materials. I think it was Appia who evolved the theory that the actor needs for contrast on the stage not rounded materials but backgrounds in opposition to his own roundness (but always three-dimensional like him)—that a very few architectural forms in linear and angular arrangement ideally set the action out.

Screens, equally abstract, and with more body, more spine, have proved themselves among the most adaptable and satisfactory devices utilized by designers who wished to abandon realistic depiction or suggestion but without adopting a purely formal or architectural stage. Occasionally the screens have served a single play, but usually the designer has experimented with a "system," built rigidly in standardized units and planned for interchangeable use with many types of production.

The screens of a "system" are usually painted in a flat tone or according to one of the broken-color formulas. They have the curtain's advantages of providing a simple and neutral background, emphasizing the actor, and offering abstract decorative possibilities; and they are more adaptable, can be rearranged in endless combinations, with extraordinarily different emotional suggestion. The best known system, and father of them all, is that designed and patented (with questionable efficacy) by Gordon Craig. At one time he considered his portable folding screens, "the thousand scenes in one scene," an answer to many of the questions he had asked about typically theatrical staging; but more recently, I think, he has been studying through to other stages, considering this an answer only in one type of production. The screen device is in wide use, however, on studio stages in both Europe and America, and occasionally finds place in the more "regular" theatres.

The inventor has described the physical features of the system as follows:*

"The scene is made up usually of four, six, eight, ten or twelve screens; and, although sometimes of more than twelve, seldom less than four. Each part or leaf of a screen is alike in every particular except breadth, and these parts together form a screen, composed of two, four, six, eight or ten leaves. These leaves fold either way and are monochrome in tint. The height of all these screens is alike.

"These screens are self-supporting and are made either of a wooden frame covered with canvas, or of solid wood.

"With screens of narrow dimensions curved forms are produced, for large rectangular spaces broader leaved screens are used, and for varied and broken forms all sizes are employed. . . .

"Sometimes certain additions may be made to this scene, such as a flight of steps, a window, a bridge, a balcony, and of course the necessary furniture, though great care and reserve must be exercised in making these additions so as to avoid the ridiculous.

"This scene is a living thing. In the hands of an artist it is capable of all varieties of expression, even as a living voice and a living face are capable of every expression. The scene remains always the same, while incessantly changing. . . .

* The article from which the quotation is taken is unsigned, but appeared in Craig's important journal of the theatre, *The Mask*.

"Through its use we obtain a sense of harmony and a sense of variety at the same time. We may be said to have recovered one of the unities of the Greek drama without losing any of the variety of the Shakespearean drama. We pass from one scene to another without a break of any kind, and when the change has come we are not conscious of any disharmony between it and that which has passed."

The one outstanding production with Craig's screens was that of *Hamlet* at the Moscow Art Theatre. There seem to have been attained in the performance a dignity and splendor very unusual, a perfect proportioning of parts, and a notable harmony of action and scene. A correspondent of the London *Times* wrote at the time: "Mr. Craig has the singular power of carrying the spiritual significance of words and dramatic situations beyond the actor to the scene in which he moves. By the simplest means he is able, in some mysterious way, to evoke almost any sensation of time or space, the scenes even in themselves suggesting variations of human emotions.

"Take, for example, the Queen's chamber in the Castle of Elsinore. Like all the other scenes, it is simply an arrangement of the screens already mentioned. There is nothing which definitely represents a castle, still less the locality or the period; and yet no one would hesitate as to its significance —and why? Because it is the spiritual symbol of such a room. A symbol, moreover, whose form is wholly dependent upon the action which it surrounds; every line, every space of light and shadow going directly to heighten and amplify the significance of that action, and becoming thereby something more than its mere setting—a vital and component part no longer separable from the whole."

In America the basic idea of Craig's scene was used in "little theatre" production by Sam Hume, most notably at the Arts and Crafts Playhouse in Detroit. His "adaptable setting" there, consisting of screens, pylons, stairs, arches and hangings, has been widely and not too intelligently taken as a model by many amateur and semi-professional acting groups. A system of this sort, with extraordinary range of possibilities for beauty when manipulated imaginatively and with taste, is so bare of ornament that it may very easily be arranged into commonplace aspects if it be handled insensitively and without an understanding of linear and mass composition. In plate 88 I am showing one arrangement of the setting on the Detroit stage. With rearrangements of the elements shown here and two additional "units" Hume set eleven plays in a single season, with far more than usual fairness to the acting and greater intrinsic beauty of scene.

The so-called "relief stage" was developed by Georg Fuchs for a special sort of conventionalized mounting that approached the screen idea. The basic theory was that if actors appear to the audience on a shallow stage, as if a flat screen and nothing more were behind them, a new decorative value could be given to their movements, and a new intimacy could be set up between players and audience. The simplification and shallow plasticity in staging thus achieved were an asset, and there were times when the sculpturesque movement of the actors—like figures in a sculptured relief-panel—seemed to have added a fresh visual appeal in the art of the theatre. The actual backgrounds, although they ranged from sheer curtains to such simple "suggestive" scenes as those famous ones by Fritz Erler for *Faust,* always threw the actor into prominence, concentrating interest where it indubitably belongs. Special attention was paid to the costuming, the movement of the actors being considered from the viewpoint of their individual places in a shifting pattern of color. With the shallow backgrounds Fuch used permanent architectural portals in an adjustable proscenium frame.

The relief-stage resulted in conventionalization and a high visual stylization. The sharp silhouetting of the figures, the decorative parade of the costumes, the closeness of the actor to the spectator, appealed to many a visiting director and artist as the accomplishment of all that Craig had hinted at; and although fortunately few designers built stages as cramped and shallow as that of Fuchs at the Munich Art Theatre, the principles of the relief-stage were absorbed into the art creed of many a German theatre; and through *Sumurun* particularly, they reached England and America.

Though his individual conception of staging thus came and went as something intangibly contributing to the march of progress, rather than as a theory persisting in its own complete form, Fuchs is placed by some critics as third of the great pioneers, with Craig and Appia. His book, *Die Revolution des Theaters,* was published in 1909 in Germany, and attained wide circulation. Even more than in his particular theory of relief staging, perhaps, there was value in his insistence upon a return from photographic imitation of life to something theatrically shaped. There is a suspicion in my mind, indeed, that there is direct opposition between the ideas of theatricalism and of shallow relief: that to use all the physical means of the theatre implies more of space and freedom than the relief stage permitted.

# IX

## THE RECORD BY NATIONS

IF this were more a book of the history of twentieth-century stagecraft, instead of an essay at setting forth primarily the various *ideas* about decoration, and their changes, it would be necessary to pause along the way to trace the chronological progress of the movement toward re-theatralization in each of the major countries. As it is, I cannot do less than mention briefly the main currents of thought and practice in the more important centers of progress. Let me begin by going back to the background against which the work of Fuchs developed in Germany, and then forward to Reinhardt and the other practicing artists; and then to France, Russia, England and America.

I have already quoted Schlegel's criticism of the scene in the early nineteenth century. Others in the full current were the architect Schinkel, Immermann, Tieck, Savits, and finally but differently Brahm. The line of thought was through merely destructive criticism of the ridiculously artificial perspective scene, to timid efforts at reviving bare stages for Shakespeare, and on to the gains made for naturalism. It was the naturalistic Brahm who ruled, with a faint counter-voice here and there advocating that the reform be turned in the direction of art rather than elaborate imitation, when Appia brought out his book, *Die Musik und die Inscenierung*, to be followed shortly by Craig with books and exhibitions. From these two the modern movement may justly be said to start here as elsewhere, and it was in Germany that it first attained the proportions of a true and effective revolution. Fuchs was obviously indebted to Craig and Appia, but added great impetus to the current. Among the notable practitioners Adolph Linnebach of the Dresden State Theatre stands out. For a long period he changed his stagecraft with the changes of thought, and contributed not a little to the mechanical advance, particularly in lighting. He is the type of regisseur that has put Germany's theatres ahead of all other national groups in testing practically the new theories of staging and in building adequate theatres, and incidentally in every one of those compromise steps which have kept the current drama dressed tastefully and within hailing distance of the real radicals. There are perhaps a score of these regisseurs of truly creative power in Germany, so that the examples of progress are to be witnessed not in the theatres of Berlin alone, but in Munich, Dresden, Weimar, Cologne, Frankfort and half a dozen other centers.

For the outside world, however, the progress in stagecraft in Germany is bound up with the name of one man, Max Reinhardt. He is the great popularizer, the great practical advocate of the newer ideas. It is impossible to discover just how much he has contributed in the field of stage decoration, because he always has worked with well-known and inventive designers. But he has grasped one idea after another and put it into practice. Beginning with the perfecting of naturalism, he went forward to simplified staging of realism, to unified suggestive methods of mounting, to striking stylization, to the formal stage in immense circus-theatre productions. And to-day, when advanced practical thought has actually caught up with Craig and Appia, Reinhardt is presenting his plays on architectural stages of the most approved sort. He has served more than any other one man as a missionary of the compromise wing of modernism, teaching England and America about new methods and new inventions before the ideas arrived in a large way by any other channel, and even finding imitators in conservative France. He has over-stylized at times, giving rise to the criticism that the new idea was to glorify stagecraft at the expense of the dramatist: he has too often overwhelmed the senses at the expense of spiritual and dramatic content. But he has staged more acceptably progressive productions than any other director. He is a genius in the organization of groups of artists, and probably some of the praise that has been his, insofar as stage decoration is concerned, should have been passed along to those artists who have worked with him, most notably Emil Orlik and Ernst Stern.

For the rest, completing this three-paragraph summary of Germany's contribution to stagecraft history, there is a group of designers whose names have gone abroad as practitioners of solidly appealing settings in simplified stylized vein: Ludwig Sievert, Knut Strom and Rochus Gliese, Fritz Schumacher, one of the earliest experimenters with abstract screen arrangements, Paul Ott, Alfred Roller, Herman Krehan, Ludwig Kainer, Emil Pirchan, of whom we shall hear more in connection with the space stage ideas of Jessner, T. C. Pillartz, Ottomar Starke, Karl Walser, Hans Strohbach, who reduces one of the most elaborate and expensively equipped stages in the world to a simple space stage, Otto Reigbert, and the Austrian Oskar Strnad. All of these men can (or could) be counted upon to supply a setting emotionally appropriate to the play, simple, decoratively attractive, satisfyingly colorful. To-day most of them are thinking in terms of space and light, or of formal architectural and space stages. With the equally progressive regisseurs with whom they work, they form the most advanced group of wide and regular practitioners in the world's theatres—and they have the most serviceable equipment of up-to-date stages to work on.

France has curiously lagged behind Germany and Russia, even behind the United States, in adopting progressive methods. The French axiom that all important art developments have their beginnings in France, and the consequent disinclination to adopt any innovation from foreign sources, have militated against acceptance (except in rare individual cases) of the ideas of Craig, Appia, Fuchs, Meyerhold and other leaders. The exceptions are Jacques Copeau and Louis Jouvet; otherwise there is very little to prove to-day that France has profited profoundly by the march of the modernist spirit in the theatre.

Long ago, in the days when Antoine was making history with the *Théâtre Libre*, freeing the playwright from encumbering traditions, he also made experiments in naturalistic stage setting, even to real stone benches, jets of water and similar wonders. There was an incipient counter-revolt in the early 'nineties, in the name of the Symbolists, an attempt to bring an almost ascetic simplicity and an aesthetic unity to the stage; and several important painters were enlisted by Lugné-Poë for his *Théâtre d'Art*, afterwards the *Théâtre de l'Oeuvre*. But the movement dissipated itself in painters' experiments, although the ideas expressed by some of the participants were in accordance with much that later went into the current of twentieth-century progressivism. The trouble in France all along, one feels, is that the reforms in the scene were merely reforms in the methods of painting. The setting was simplified, but the designer was practicing decorative painting in place of the old detail painting—when what was needed was to get away from the painter's conception altogether.

After the experiments of painters as prominent as Maurice Denis and Bonnard, under Lugné-Poë and Paul Fort, there was an unaccountably long dead period: the very time when the rest of Europe was awakening to the importance of the ideas advanced by Appia and Craig. It was not until 1910 that a new wave of interest set in, when Jacques Rouché, later to become director of the conservative Paris Opera, published a book called *l'Art Théatral Moderne*, in which he summarized his observations of the staging of plays in the theatres of Fuchs, Reinhardt, Stanislavsky and Meyerhold, and reviewed at length the books of Craig and Appia. In the same year Rouché established the *Théâtre des Arts* in Paris, and prepared, as one French writer* put it, "to fix the principles of the new stagecraft in accordance with the French genius." Again a group of painters very important and very progressive were called in to collaborate, and again the scene was bettered—but remained essentially a painters' plaything. Even to-day the experiments that are most hailed by the art magazines and dramatic journals in France are those which are bringing the painters Picasso, Derain, Matisse, Laurencin and Braque temporarily to stage work; exceptionally interesting individual occasions, and fruitful of important bits, but hardly on the high-road to a truly modern *theatre*.

Valdo Barbey developed a style of flat background painting which left the actors well in relief, counting on the costuming to afford a color pattern; Maxime Dethomas and Drésa attempted valiantly to get beyond the paint "feel" to something more solid and plastic; Gemier staged some productions too obviously derived from Reinhardt; but it has been the artists grouped around the exotic Russian Ballet who alone have given Paris real thrills over the changes in stagecraft, with painty stuff.

France enjoyed leadership in the world theatre so long, in the older eras, and is so sensitive, so keen, in all that concerns art, that the truly theatrical ideal cannot help but make headway there: the ideas of world leaders elsewhere are bound to be absorbed before long. But the delay has puzzled many a student of the stage. Two artists alone seem to have carried the

* Léon Moussinac: *la Décoration Théatrale.* Paris, 1922.

new spirit at its finest into France, Copeau and Jouvet, and of them I shall speak at length in connection with the story of the still emerging formal stage.

England must be credited with Gordon Craig's contribution to modernism, for after all he was almost literally born on the British stage, played on it for years, as child and actor, and in British productions found both the entrenched artificiality and stupidity against which he later revolted, and the impulse to rebellion. But there is little besides Craig's beginnings to record to the country's account on the world's stage decoration ledger. Not so much insular as bull-headedly independent, England insisted on holding to tradition, giving way to one step after another in reform of current staging years after other countries were experimenting and accomplishing. Having exiled Craig by disbelief and neglect, London held to the realistic and archaeological modes, particularly as they persisted under Beerbohm Tree, until that day when Granville Barker rediscovered Craig's principles as "made practical" by Germany and Reinhardt. Barker as regisseur drew into his service the two men who have since become, aside from Craig, almost the only British artists internationally known as stage decorators: Norman Wilkinson and Albert Rutherston. Both remain a little too much decorators, rather than designers of stages; but both have done solidly simple settings, prettily stylized, and both have given impetus to the rather feeble anti-realism current. Charles Ricketts has been less active, but did pioneer work, and Lovat Fraser was just breaking into stage designing with a jolly sort of conventionalization at the time of his regrettable death. For the rest, there were continuous experiments at the Everyman Theatre under Norman Macdermott, and at the Birmingham Repertory Theatre under Barry V. Jackson; and more important, the researches and rare productions of William Poel brought to light many illuminating facts about the Elizabethan stage. Paul Nash is the only artist whose coming to the theatre in the last five years has seemed to promise exceptionally fine accomplishment. The story might almost be summed up in Craig, Barker, Nash.

In this rapid roll-call of the nations and their contributions, I am not more than mentioning Russia here, because the very important developments in that country have seemed to demand individual treatment as theories or accomplishment in particular fields: the Bakst-Benois-Anisfeld development as example of glorified painting on the dance and opera stages; Stanislavsky and the Moscow Art Theatre as an interesting counter-current to theatricalism; Meyerhold as an individual theorist; and Tairoff and fellow experimenters as contributors to the stream of Expressionism. It is impossible, too, for such a brief essay to mention more than the name of H. T. Wijdeveld as leader of a group of theorists who see radically and clearly in Holland; or the Capeks and K. H. Hilar in Czecho-Slovakia, although a student of stagecraft might learn much in a week in Prague; or René Moulaert as an accomplished director and decorator in Belgium. Vienna is very much an outpost of German progressivism, and one of the foremost cities of the world, theatrically considered. Italy has been galvanized into consideration of the future of the stage by the startling experiments of a group of radicals headed by the father of Futurism, Marinetti, and the designers Bragaglia and Prampolini. Of them we shall hear more in connection with the extreme forms of Expressionism.

In treating the "new movement" in America, I want to go into a little more detail, because this is my own country and the American theatre my own field, and this book is a part of what we are trying to do and to make clear to each other. Be it said at once, the creative sources of the modern theatre, so far as it has developed here, are largely to be sought elsewhere. We have creative artists who early absorbed the principles of Craig and Appia, and then went forward with admirable independence. But there was no figure that measured near the stature of these two, not even a student with the perception of William Poel or a mechanic with the genius of a Linnebach. It is only within the last five years that there has emerged work strikingly original enough to attract the attention of the world, in the projects of Geddes and Jones.

The conjunction of forces that brought about a very flowering of pretty stagecraft between 1915 and 1920 was due to the meeting of several impulses from Europe. Within a year or two of the earlier date, America saw the Viennese Joseph Urban introduce simplified and extraordinarily decorative mounting to the opera in Boston, saw Winthrop Ames import the Reinhardt production of *Sumurun,* saw Granville Barker bring over productions with decorations by Norman Wilkinson and Albert Rutherston, saw Robert Edmond Jones return to America from study with Reinhardt, saw Sam Hume return after working in Gordon Craig's studio-school in Italy, to organize America's first exhibition of modern stagecraft. Behind the wide acceptance of and response to this series of importations, there was a background of a great dissatisfaction with the over-commercialization of the professional theatre, and a very live interest in non-traditional staging at the colleges and universities, expressing itself largely in open-air productions and on revived stages, and timidly reaching out to grasp at Craig's ideas as set down in his first book. The earliest little theatres, amateur and semi-professional organizations born out of the dual impulses of protest and self-expression, were already taking faltering steps toward simplification and tastefulness.

The first burst of activity came in the little theatres, which multiplied almost unbelievably in the course of two years. The new stagecraft became a passion with the directors and artists of these "outside" theatres, and there speedily developed a group of "decorators" with keen sensibility, imagination and talent. The Washington Square Players in New York brought to the fore Lee Simonson and Rollo Peters, the Los Angeles Little Theatre gave Norman-Bel Geddes a chance to prove his exceptional ability, Livingston Platt began to be talked about for his settings at the Toy Theatre in Boston, and Raymond Jonson was doing obviously new and appealing things on the tiny stage of the Chicago Little Theatre under the tutelage of Maurice Browne. At the same time Robert Edmond Jones found his way to the larger stage on Broadway, and Urban continued his work for both opera and legitimate production. On this foundation there developed during the following five years a professional group of stage designers who were soon showing more creative ability, more vision and more solid knowledge of the art of the theatre than were the actors, playwrights or directors with whom they worked; and new men were being graduated continually from the little theatres. The entry of the United States into the world war closed many of the amateur playhouses for a season or two; but it is a sign of the fundamental soundness and strength of the new spirit that the progressive work was so soon picked up again without serious loss of impetus.

The New York shows were being dressed up in the loveliest of clothes, whether they deserved them or not, and the little theatres were staging their endless productions with a finish, a daring and a physical appeal that ten years earlier would have seemed magic. The thoroughness with which the commercial theatre was won over to the simplified stagecraft—though without fundamental change in type of play or stage—was in itself an indication that the artists concerned were compromising the principles they took from Craig, were setting aside the deeper vision several of them had seen of an entirely different theatre. As in Europe, in New York the artists applied first a process of simplification, then came to simplicity with suggestion, embraced pictorial design, and finally arrived at stylization—where, indeed, most of them pause to-day.

In treating this progress in its larger aspects, I have already said that the change for the better was remarkable, and the visual prettiness of staging in workaday productions immeasurably increased, wherever the new spirit was at work; but that the movement as a whole was a compromise. I do not want to say more than this for the American group alone.

What I would like to convey is this: in a theatre creatively dead, committed to a tradition of naturalistic staging, the designers stepped in and in one department created an independent beauty, at the same time giving consideration to the acting and dramatic values insofar as they counted; but they were not the uncompromising artists, clinging to their vision and ideals in a way that moves worlds. In a "reasonable" conservative view, they accomplished a revolution; in a radical view, they made safe and pretty something that were better abandoned, seldom more than touching over into the field of the living future.

It may be that I am imposing my own personal judgment too harshly here: I have come to a firm belief that ultimately the theatre will abandon almost entirely the realistic mode, will develop a stage almost as far from the current proscenium-frame peep-hole affair as were the Greek and Elizabethan platforms; that imitation and finish will give way as ideals, before expressive form and emotional intensification; that the theatre must return to an identity of its own and not remain a servile if interesting portrayer of surface life. You, dear reader, may well discount my opinion, since in the immediate view, and as ninety-nine out of a hundred critics and students see the case, these artists we have been considering have rescued the stage in your town and mine from evils of false artificiality and over-detailed photography; have brought it up from a region where incompetence and negligence reigned to a place where mechanical efficiency lives, and reasonable taste. To do so much, I freely agree, is a considerable feat.

The men concerned in this upward march are still to be found in two groups, the larger consisting of the professional theatre workers, on that Broadway which beckons the artist with considerable gold, and with the lure of opportunity to display his wares along the most active and gaudiest street in the amusement world; and in the little theatres.

Those who have had most to do with bringing the commercial stage up to its present well-dressed standard are the pioneers Joseph Urban, Robert Edmond Jones, Norman-Bel Geddes and Lee Simonson, and over as long a period but less actively, Rollo Peters, Livingston Platt, Hermann Rosse, Claude Bragdon and John Wenger; and more recently Woodman Thompson, Cleon Throckmorton, James Reynolds, Mordecai Gorelik, Sheldon K. Viele, Donald Oenslager, Frederick Jones, Jo Mielziner, Aline Bernstein, B. Aronson, Raymond Sovey and Ernest deWeerth. The list would somehow seem incomplete without mention of Robert Bergman, whose unique understanding of the technical problems of building and painting has been an immeasurable aid to the progressive designers.

Of the artists working in the little theatres and community theatres out through the country, sometimes in a miniature mirroring of the best accomplishment in New York, sometimes with greater daring and more interesting results, one cannot mention more than the pioneers Sam Hume and Irving Pichel, both traveling close to abstraction and formality in staging; and such type figures as Robert R. Sharpe of the Pasadena Community Playhouse, Jonel Jorgelesco of the Boston Repertory Theatre and B. Aronson of the Bronx *Unser Theater*.

Out of the total group of practicing artists it is difficult to pick individuals and say that these are the men who will shape the future of stage decoration in America, who will throw off the compromise habit and the limitations of realism and aid creatively in shaping the theatre of to-morrow.

But it would be a blind spectator who failed to single out Norman-Bel Geddes as the possessor of the most vivid imagination in the American professional theatre, unbridled at times but gloriously far-riding at others; or Robert Edmond Jones as the most sensitive and thorough-going experimenter in new forms, with a real beauty springing out of everything he touches, in traditional or visionary fields. Hermann Rosse has long been pushing against the bars set up by custom, and Lee Simonson has been constantly alert to try out new methods as he has observed them during his world-roaming. Then, too, there are the still younger men dreaming non-realistic dreams—of whom I can speak only as I have happened to know the projects of certain individuals. Among them I feel that Gorelik, Oenslager and Aronson particularly are refusing to be bound to past times or the present theatre. But then, America, young, pushing, eager, feverish, experiencing, dreaming, pouring untold wealth and energy into what passes for the arts, may thereby turn up who knows what surprises, what glories? Already Geddes has startled others beside his own countrymen.

# X

## SQUARING THE NEW STAGING WITH EXPRESSIONISM

EXPRESSIONISM in stage decoration and in play production means many things to many people (as doubtless does realism), due to the common confusion in art terminology. For me Expressionism includes all those methods that look to greater intensification of dramatic emotion, to greater theatrical expressiveness, as against those that are designed to imitate life with faithful detail, that give back an interesting representation of actuality. When one shapes his decoration with the double object of aiding concentration on the theatric reality or dramatic "flow" of the production, and of contributing by every physical and visual virtue of the stage to the theatrical "form," then he is being Expressionistic.

Like the Expressionist painter, who is less interested in the actuality of the object than in some essential quality of structural truth he has divined in it, and then in expressing his own emotion over that, and finally in wrapping all this in some sort of creative "form" that capitalizes and intensifies all the particular values of paint and canvas; so the new stage director or designer tries to foster an inner truth or quality or rhythm that is in the poet's script, by emotional rather than imitative means, and by utilizing those special things that belong to the stage. The painter no longer tries to hide the paint-and-canvas look in order to make his picture more like a photograph. He declares the flatness of his canvas and glories in the paint as such. So the clear-sighted worker in the modern theatre will come more and more to declare his theatre: he will not hide the acting platform behind a curtain in order to flash into sudden view a true surface picture of an actual place, but will develop his stage formally and decoratively, nursing its essentially theatric virtues.

Expressionism in this sense covers all that is being accomplished in the march toward abstraction in setting, toward formal stages and space stages; it finds its great pioneers, so far as the theatre is concerned, in Appia and

Craig; it extends through the experiments of a dozen world figures into regions still too speculative and dim for us ordinary mortals to follow.

But what people too often mean when they exclaim, "I don't like Expressionist scenery," is that they have seen plays staged before Expressionist *paintings*—and the obvious inappropriateness set their teeth on edge, just as it does yours and mine. It is probably true that nine-tenths of all the productions which were reported as experiments in mounting plays Expressionistically between 1915 and 1925 were examples of more or less unrealistic dramas (mostly old plays written before the reign of realism) placed in settings that were merely transferences of the mannerisms of radical painting. Expressionistic painting has no more place on the stage than has Impressionistic or naturalistic, or the old muddy nineteenth-century sort that even the easel painters could give no adequately descriptive name.

There were many and widely discussed examples of the "new art" thus brought to the stage around 1920, chiefly in Russia and Germany—although America too had its timid pioneers.* Finally the film called *The Cabinet of Dr. Caligari* took the fame of Expressionism as a mode of setting around the world. It was a marvelous technical achievement, and in most of its scenes it harmonized actor and background effectively. But the settings, with deformity of nature emphasized largely by means of paint on canvas, were adequate to the brief and swiftly changing scenes of the moving picture where they would only prove over-stimulating, eccentric and irritating when set before an audience for an entire act of a play. The mode there employed was in its own place direct, expressive, convincing; but the designers for the legitimate stage who grasped the outward trick of the manner gave us only startling and immediately effective things where quietly expressive and soundly theatric things were needed. Artists who had left the older sorts of painted setting safely behind years before, suddenly gave way to the impulse to try on a new style in painting. It was as if one might try to make one's old buggy or one's new automobile more modern by tracing a cubistic design or copying an Expressionistic scene on the outside of it. Expressionism really must begin with the innards.

It should be remembered here that although the men who had simplified

* See Kenneth Macgowan's *The Theatre of Tomorrow*, New York, 1921, Chapter VIII.

and stylized the current realistic setting had learned that a too close adherence to nature was disillusioning, that an extremely lifelike representation drew too much attention to itself on account of the very perfection of the imitation, nevertheless they did not so drastically simplify or so ruthlessly reshape nature that the scene might not seem reasonably like a bit taken out of real life somewhere. While avoiding the danger of reproducing life too accurately, they likewise avoided violating nature as seen by the so-called normal eye. One of the first freedoms claimed by the Expressionists had to do with this limitation. They claimed the right to violate, deform and reshape outward nature just as far as such violence furthered emotional expressiveness. Distortion became a rule of the first Expressionist painters and earmarked the whole movement as decadent in the minds of all those who consider fidelity of imitation the first test of art. And it is distortion, or perhaps "detachment"—not of the painter's kind—that most clearly outwardly marks Expressionistic work in the theatre.

In stage decoration ("decoration" has become a *very* unserviceable word here) it may be that the designer throws over allegiance to natural aspect in order to gain expressiveness through rearrangements of motifs out of nature, or through abstract manipulation of line, mass and color in the surrounding walls of a setting; or it may be that he transfers the play out of any mounting in built-up backgrounds to a formal stage, a platform that remains permanently and confessedly an acting platform and not a framework for picture scenes; or perhaps he aims at the nearest achievable approximation to a toe-hold in absolute space. But detachment from nature is at the bottom of all these methods.

Despite my own belief in our ultimate arrival at the formal stage or a space stage, I cannot hurdle all the attempts to apply the principles of modernism to the surface setting, to flat surrounding backgrounds for stage action. My illustrations include experiments in grasping the principles of abstract graphic art and adapting them to scene making. The setting for *The Makropoulos Secret* as worked out for the Pasadena Community Playhouse by Robert R. Sharpe seems quite clearly to have been inspired by that same wing of the German Expressionist painters to which the collaborators on *Dr. Caligari* made their bow. As a matter of record I include also a scene from the *Caligari* film (plate 92).

Another group of modernists brought a different mode of painting to the theatre, and almost convinced even the most uncompromising formalists that it belonged by right there. Those artists who reacted from realism in the direction of a child-like or primitive *naïveté*, contributed particularly to the staging of the Russian and Swedish Ballets in Paris, and to the famous *Soirées de Paris* in 1924. In some measure the simplicity and clarity of this type of painted setting may be considered a reaction from the hot intensity and elaboration of the earlier ballet setting under the influence of Bakst; but the greater reason is in the fact that Derain, Matisse, Picasso, Dufy, and others of those called upon, were artists who had been nurtured on Primitivism and had come to an engaging and decorative simplicity in their painting, and when faced with a theatrical problem that could be met with painted curtains in similar vein, their response was a sort of enlarged naïve easel picture. In some cases the mode was perfectly in place, and the audiences enjoyed individual exhibitions of extraordinary charm and other-worldliness. But as a contribution to progress in stagecraft, these widely heralded experiments, though brought forth by the most talented group of painters in the world to-day, hardly touched more than the fringe of the problem.

Derain's curtains for *la Boutique Fantasque* were typical examples, with a Rousseau-like fancy given full play; and Jean Hugo's *Roméo et Juliette* ballet setting was as simple as an unspoiled child might make it. The same note was apparent in the works contributed by Matisse, Gontcharova, Foujita, Picasso, Larionoff, Leger and Dufy. The settings of all these show the true Expressionist disregard for nature "as is."

*Sur-réalism* seems to me a matter of surface Expressionism, however deep down in their beings the artists find their inspiration, and it is not likely to affect staging profoundly unless the principles are applied primarily to the conception of the play. So too the systems of those painters who design in total abstraction, with pattern-pictures of undeniable if puzzling appeal. Their stage backgrounds, as worked out for instance by the Bauhaus group in Dessau, have elemental simplicity and precise formal qualities, but apparently not in particular a dramatic value as background to the moving actor.

The Italians have recently been very active in the search for new scenic equivalents. The Futurist group, always devoted to the machine, looking to it for inspiration and utilizing its characteristics in design, have invaded the stage and have tried out abstract and mechanistic methods. Before them, perhaps, Achille Ricciardi conceived of a color accompaniment for setting as an expressional aid to drama, following the action with a changing pattern of colored light, a shade for every nuance of emotion, time or place. He here touched on a truth in the understanding of which we are, perhaps, veriest amateurs. But any such over-use of *change* in lighting as he evidently indulged in could hardly avoid being intrusive. Abstraction pursued in that direction may yield up other glories which we have but half imagined, as an independent art like Thomas Wilfred's "mobile color"; but that implies a "theatre" of a distinctive sort with little relation to the great tradition of acted drama.* Anton Giuglio Bragaglia would, if I understand his object, follow out Craig's ideas of movement and theatricality on stages such as we have known, but with a new machine-age glorification of scenic elements. He writes:† "With us the prose theatre is less interesting than the musical theatre, as the former has become all representation with very little of the spectacle. In Italy, particularly, the theatre of the great tradition is essentially and vividly spectacular. . . . The future playwrights will be able to do something when furnished with original scenic mediums for constructive creations. That is to say when the stage is mated with the movie art. Mechanical scenery, mysterious and powerful muse, can alone inspire new methods of spectacles, characteristic of our own modern times. —And machinery will not betray poetry. On the contrary! With modern rhythms, poetry will sing vivid, miraculous apparitions of the scenic prism of the ten faces. Life, varied in its myriads of pictures will then and only then be presented in the simultaneous synthesis of its panorama. . . . *Mod-*

* I have found no translation of Ricciardi's book, *Il teatro del Colore*. The reader interested in "mobile color" will find a chapter on the subject, with illustrations, in my book, *A Primer of Modern Art*, New York, 1924.

† "The Theatrical Theatre," in *The Little Review*, winter number, 1926.

*ern reform intends to return to theatrical machinery its ancient prestige, which procured so many successes, triumphs and glories for the genial and ingenious work of our scenic artists.*"

I confess to being a little vague about the concrete means intended by Bragaglia; and the photographs I have seen of his settings indicate merely a plastic practice within the starkly simplified picture stage, with more than usual leaning toward abstract composition in line and volume. But perhaps it is only because he is forced to associate with old-fashioned literary playwrights, there being no Futurist ones worthy the name, that he fails to transform the stage with new spectacular glories of the machine age.

Enrico Prampolini, of the same group of Italian radicals, goes one step farther, and pins his faith to "scenic dynamism" and to "space as a *scenic personality* dominating theatrical action"; and he finally arrives at the "Polyexpressive and Magnetic Theatre," a theatre without actors and without a stage. When he still utilized a stage, his designs were not unlike those of the surface abstractionists. Even then they were more interesting as steps toward a "theatre of mechanics" than as contributions to the solution of contemporary dramatic problems. Some of his statements, however (in the same issue of the *Little Review*), are arresting and provocative of thought:

"With the *abolition* of the *stage* and the 'scenic-arc' the technical possibilities of theatrical action find broader scope outside the three-dimensional terms of tradition. By dividing the horizontal surface by new vertical oblique and polydimensional elements, by forcing the cubic resistance of the 'scenic-arc' by the spheric expansion of plastic planes moving rhythmically in space, we arrive at the *creation of a polydimensional and futuristic scenic space*. . . .

"I consider the actor a *useless element* in theatrical action and moreover one that is dangerous to the future of the theatre. . . . We are tired of seeing this grotesque rag of humanity agitating itself futilely under the vast dome of the stage in an effort to stimulate its own emotions. The appearance of the human element on the *stage*, destroys the mystery *of the beyond*, which must rule in the theatre, a temple of spiritual abstraction. . . .

"From painting, *sceno-synthesis*, to plastic, *sceno-plastic*, from this to the architecture of plastic planes in movement, sceno-dynamic. From the traditional three dimensional scene to the creation of *polydimensional scenic-space*, from the human actor to the new scenic personality of space, the actor, from this to the *polyexpressive magnetic theatre;* which I see already outlined architectonically in the center of a valley of spiral terraces, *dynamic hills* on which rise bold constructions of *polydimensional scenic-space, center* of irradiation of the futuristic atmospheric scenery."

However interested we may be in plastic values *per se* and in scenic imagination, we seem here to have got beyond stage decoration in the sense in which I chose the term for the title of this book. I am frankly writing about changes in the *platform for acting,* and I therefore leave further pursuit of Prampolini's soaring ideas to those who are prepared to abandon the actor and to transform the stage into a super-human performing machine among the "dynamic hills." I likewise somewhat reluctantly omit the sweepingly new conceptions of Frederick Kiesler for the optophonic theatre and for stages swimming in space.

There have been many attempts to capitalize the values of *moving* scenery, but in the sort of theatre we are holding to, it seems to me that movement in the settings, however carefully designed to be in keeping, cannot prove other than an interruption of the spectator's preoccupation with the dramatic story, other than a distraction. I am open to conviction—but I have never seen it work out in practice or experiment, and I cannot visualize it. Stillness seems to me a vital element of setting, as it does of noble architecture. But when scenery becomes the chief actor, then I shall withdraw my objection.

Vesvolod Meyerhold has led the sanely insurgent forces in the Russian theatre, and I think that the stability of his position has been due largely to the fact that he always held, in his theories and his experiments, to the importance of the actor in the performance as seen by an audience. He was once a worker with Stanislavsky and Nemirovitch-Danchenko at the Moscow Art Theatre, but he early differed with them about the conservative methods of stage setting at that most important playhouse. Stanislavsky throughout his career has seen further intensification of the actor's expressiveness as the chief aim of "art theatre" technique. His company, probably the most remarkable acting machine in the world during the height of the realistic era, went beyond imitative playing, reaching a style and an achievement sometimes termed a "spiritualized realism." Without attempting a difficult analysis here, I may say that in a sense they went through and beyond realism to a psychologically true region where there was much of that clarity, emotional directness and expressiveness which the radicals are attempting to attain by throwing aside imitative methods—instead of reaching through them to something approaching imitation of the soul. In the matter of settings, however, the Moscow Art Theatre, except in the very rare instances of a *Blue Bird* or a *Hamlet* in Craig's screens, was content with the contemporary fashion. Even when the theatre became a world-famous model of progressiveness in acting, its stage decoration remained in general old-fashioned and not even the best of the traditional kind. This devotion to the old stuff hardly constituted a serious counter-current to modernism—as, for instance, did the Bakst pursuit of the glorified painty setting—for it was not followed with any particular conviction. Stanislavsky, to be sure, came nearer to revealing the soul of man in acting than any previous director, but he saw no inappropriateness in building his settings of the sort of meaningless details that he had instinctively dropped from his playing—and Meyerhold, most clear-sighted of all Russian theorists about stage setting, seceded from the Art Theatre company.

Meyerhold held to acting as the most important element of production, but he went about emphasizing it on the stage by throwing over all allegiance to naturalness in the setting. He wanted above all else to bring the actors before the audience disembarrassed of casual nature. It was in connection with his experiments that the first wave of discussion about "the theatre theatrical" broke over the critical world. At first, after leaving the Art Theatre, he developed the idea of the relief stage—bringing his actors forward. From this he conceived some notion of further tying together the actors and the audience, partially by decoration (or the form of the stage) and lights. He soon did away with the proscenium curtain, and relegated to a small area at the back of the stage such changes in the suggestion of reality as still seemed necessary. He even kept the auditorium lights up during the performance in an effort to make the spectators feel that they were part of the life of the theatre, rather than merely paid entrants at the photographic exhibition of a bit out of natural life.

Later Meyerhold not only abandoned the curtain but eliminated the proscenium arch. His stage became literally and nakedly a platform for acting; or rather a series of platforms, because he found diversified movement such an effective medium. Finally he became one of the originators of the Constructivist setting.

I have thus treated Meyerhold's progress somewhat at length because he, more steadily in practice and more sanely in theory than any other worker, developed the ideas inherent in the writings of Craig and Appia from mere revolt against realistic methods to creation of wholly Expressionistic methods. He is the key figure with whom we turn to the last division of my subject: the stage in space as distinguished from the setting conceived as three walls of background.

## XI

## THE MODERN STAGES

IN taking up consideration of the most readily recognized of the typically theatrical stages, as developed by the modern experimentalists, it is well to remind the reader of the excursion made in my opening pages into the subject of general theories of theatre art, and to repeat that only an understanding of the agitation for a *presentational* type of drama, as against the representational, can explain the contemporary swing toward the declared stage and the purely functional setting. In taking three types of stage for particular study—or perhaps, more properly speaking, in trying to crowd what seem to me the truly theatrical or expressive stages into a classification of three sorts—I am being entirely arbitrary.

We have here come to a new way of thinking of the stage and its "decoration": the conception of stage as *space*—something for the actor to walk on beneath, to be sure, a floor or platforms or skeleton constructions, but more important, the central acting space emphasized *instead of* the walls or background surrounding that space. We have reached here the truly and consistently plastic and tri-dimensional Expressionistic thing, with more than a vague reach toward fourth-dimensional values.

Of all the theatres designed or manipulated to bring the acting space up and forward into view, to disengage from surrounding life a bit of frankly theatrical playing space, there seem to me three type sorts: (1) the naked, outstanding carpentered stage, commonly called the "formal stage"; (2) the "space stage," which minimizes the architecture or carpentry, and attempts to arrive as close as possible to a lighted void; and (3) the Constructivist stage, with a skeleton construction in space, designed purely functionally for each new play. The boundaries between these types must be considered very elastic, to be pulled over at times so that certain examples cut into two fields. And yet the three sorts are emerging clearly enough to afford a basis for description and discussion.

The likenesses, the characteristics that warrant grouping the three sorts together, that mark them as coördinate phases, are these: all three are outgrowths of the search for a stage emphasizing the actor and action above all else. This marks them off from the older stage where the picture shared interest with the acting; and, in the other direction, from the machine-age theatres of Kiesler and Prampolini, where the actor and the playing space disappear amid moving constructions. All three are not only anti-photographic but anti-pictorial, gaining their decorative values not from a framed and arranged composition in the flat, but primarily out of movement and light, and in one division, out of permanent architectural elements. They all are entirely negligent of the representative visual values, have no facilities for a faithful reproduction of natural scenes. (The vague intimation of real places, the suggestion of locale, is not only possible but usual, absolute isolation from life, like absolute abstraction, being probably impossible and certainly undesirable with the types of drama we now know.) In all three stages the curtain either is eliminated or has become a mere occasional convenience: for changes of backgrounds and accessories are minimized, and there is seldom occasion to blot out one picture suddenly or to reveal another with the element of surprise—the essential stage or shaped void is always undisguisedly before the audience. All three rely on light, on atmospheric quality and color and light-and-shade composition, as a major resource for dramatic effect.

The unlikenesses, the differences that characterize each type, are these: the formal stage is a playing space determined by a permanent architectural platform, a carpentered platform standing out naked. This platform sometimes joins a wall at the back, and sometimes walls at the sides, but these walls, if present, are in their main elements unchangeable and immovable—not decorations. There is no proscenium arch and only a supplementary curtain part way up-stage, if any. The stage, always before the audience and therefore a permanent reminder of the theatre as theatre, may have noble decorative value in its physical form, like any other architectural composition; but its range of decorative variation is limited to a non-imitative sort.

The space stage, on the other hand, puts forward no declared platform. Its floor, indeed, is usually the same stage floor that the older theatre has known for a quarter of a century past, and the stage box the same barn-like place of old (though unseen), with proscenium arch as often as not still in place on the audience side. What links this physical stage with the modernist types is its use, not as an area surrounded with decorations but as a shaped volume of space, with surroundings suppressed as far as possible to afford the impression of a void, into which the action is placed and picked out with light. Since background cannot always be pushed back into dead darkness, the space is ordinarily surrounded by the most retiring materials: black curtains, or a cyclorama or dome from which direct lighting is carefully excluded. In this box full of space a spot in the center, on the flat floor or on successive platforms or tilted planes, is lighted—with perhaps an upright line or a column showing as an anchor in reality. Living light and movement are the basic elements of decoration.

The Constructivist stage differs from the space stage in being essentially a structure in space rather than an emphasized void. It differs from the formal stage in that there is no formal platform for acting, but a fresh construction designed to meet the needs of each play. This is, in effect, a skeleton erected in a space stage, an arranged patchwork of stripped stairs, arches, ramps, platforms, ladders, etc. There is nothing in a true Constructivist setting that is not specifically called for by the acting directions, no element that has not a definite function in utilitarian service to the players, or as scaffolding holding those elements together. The utter Constructivists, moreover, are consciously "anti-decorative," insisting that any shaping of the construction for aesthetic values is a betrayal of the theatrical values.

# XII

## THE ARCHITECTURAL STAGE

THE formal standing-out stage, the architecturally pleasing platform for acting, pushed up and forward into easy view of the audience, disembarrassed of the proscenium arch and its encumbering machinery, seems the most logical and most direct answer to the cry for more intense capitalization of the means that belong typically to the theatre as an art. It is the true answer to the call for a *plastic* stage in harmony with the plastic actor, for it is always and wholly "in the round."

This platform was in other days the setting for all drama. In Greece, in mediaeval Europe, in Elizabethan England, in old and modern Asia, it has been the scene during the greatest flowerings of dramatic art. In bringing it into the theatre again—or rather in shaping a new theatre about its essential form—the modernists are breaking with one tradition only to revive another which is older and more noble. But they also bring resources to make the revived platform more usable for acting, more flexible, more susceptible to decorative nuances.

In Greece its decorative value was in the architectural background, the noble *skene* and *paraskenia*. In Rome, one feels, these walls were too decorative in the surface sense, too ornamental: the use, acting, was being forgotten in the desire for display. The Elizabethan stage was nearer naked construction; and probably vaguely pleasing as background. The modern formal stage has all the possibilities of these others, and very many more, because its architectural values, without losing their serenity and unobtrusive decorativeness, can be heightened and made to contribute to performance values by the quiet marvels of modern lighting.

The first reason for this type of theatre, however, is that the audiences, if the director's non-realistic intent is made clear through the frank formalism of the playing space, will accept the convention of one stage remaining throughout the many scenes of a play, throughout many plays; that a declared platform for acting, obviously without means for changing its own character, without facilities for picturing many places in nature, will not be expected by the audience so to change, or to give back a view of natural surroundings. Instead the imagination of the spectator will supply new backgrounds insofar as needed. The theory even goes farther: it says—with profound truth, I believe—that in freeing the audience-mind from picture-recognition, one concentrates interest on the playing and the play; that making the setting almost wholly unreal, one intensifies the reality of that inner core of drama that speaks to the soul.

The practical advantages of a scene in which the main elements remain unchanged are too obvious to bear discussion, particularly in view of the vast amount of energy and inventiveness expended since 1890 in developing machinery to accomplish changes of setting expeditiously. No amount of perfectly functioning machinery can make possible the swiftness of scene succession, and the consequent sense of unified action, that comes with the adoption of the formal stage and the convention of one architectural scene standing for all scenes in nature. A second practical gain is the extraordinary freedom for movement, the increased decorative possibilities of the group action on a stage disentangled from the former picture accessories.

One may fairly ask how far the director, granted that he wants this general nudity, can wisely fall back on the *suggestion* of locale in individual scenes. Great variety of atmosphere is possible through the new flexibility of lighting alone. Changes in color, architectural emphasis, and even in the apparent shape of the stage, can thus be compassed. Beyond that, a very few properties, a screen or two, minor hangings, adaptable panels, are commonly utilized for indications of called-for places. If the artist can retain the sense of the stage and at the same time afford an intimation of a particular scene, or a formal conventionalization of its essential character as it might be imagined by an artist uninterested in actuality, that may be the happiest solution. Roger Fry, writing of a stage designer, once spoke of the "power of using form and color with a double meaning, first as pure design, and secondly as a means of evoking vague suggestions and flavors of time and place." Certainly if the designer can preserve the abstract values of his formal stage, and at the same time "evoke vague suggestions and flavors," he will have kept a just balance of convention and intimated reality.

For examples of modern formal stages actually built, one must go back to Jacques Copeau's *Théâtre du Vieux Colombier* in Paris, an architectural arrangement based on Elizabethan models, as the most famous; and to the shaped stages that Norman-Bel Geddes has designed for certain produced plays like *Jehanne d'Arc* and *Arabesque*, supplemented by models for unproduced plays like *Dante* and *The Mother of Christ*, which I shall call "sculptured stages"; and to Reinhardt's almost bare platforms on which he has used screens so freely. The truth is that there have been no examples of permanent formal stages built ideally, as the designers would desire them if unembarrassed by questions of money and expediency. Copeau's theatre was the best that he could crowd into a cramped and uncompromising hall (and the similar Marais Theatre in Brussels and the Elizabethan Maddermarket Theatre in England were rearranged from older stages), whereas Reinhardt continues to divide his time between proscenium-frame commercial theatres and temporary erections at Salzburg and the compromise ballroom theatre at Vienna.

Even in its non-ideal form, the stage of the *Vieux Colombier* has proved over a period of years the nearest to a perfectly responsive non-naturalistic platform for acting that the modern Western world has seen. The physical characteristics are indicated in the "opened" drawing by Louis Jouvet (plate 97) much more accurately than I could describe them. Particularly to be noted are the fore-stage, the steps to the higher stage, the permanent character of this main concrete platform, the permanent doors at stage-right, the rear wall with its built-in balcony. In the picture of the stage as set for a production, plate 98, the lanterns used for lighting are shown; and properly they are not disguised—as part of the theatre, they are built into the composition and are frankly declared as integral to it.

Copeau and Louis Jouvet, the very talented and clear-sighted actor-designer who worked with him, manipulated this stage with the slightest of changes and additions for the production of an amazingly wide repertory of plays. The illustrations indicate how little was added to dress the scene for any given production. A screen here, an outstanding property there, or a change of a panel or two on the wall, constituted the extent of the "decoration," even though the range of the drama covered practically every type of play in and out of the realistic field. Through it all the main features of the stage remained the same: the playing space was always forward and there was never any vista or decorative display beyond it to draw the attention away. The neutral stage played up constantly to the actor and the flow of action. It admirably fulfilled Copeau's expectations in that it provided a "site" for the action instead of a *décor*. It gave him "atmosphere" and "evocation."

I may add that while I have admired the work of Copeau and Jouvet greatly, I do not believe that this theatre, or this type of theatre, has yet been utilized to its full measure of beauty and expressiveness. The theory of Copeau that everything must be shaped for the actor primarily, is one to which every modernist readily subscribes. But it seems to me that after neutralizing and formalizing his stage for acting's sake, Copeau was negligent at times in the ways in which he made the minor readjustments from play to play, and particularly in the failure to utilize the abstract values of color and lighting with more appropriateness. These are thoroughly theatrical expressive means, and belong to this bare stage particularly. In the production of *Twelfth Night*, for instance, I thought the faint indications of locale commonplace where they might have been naïvely suggestive—the bare stage would have been better; and at times in other performances the revealment of careless or unfinished details in the stage area jarred as out of keeping with the spirit of thorough workmanship—which must obtain whether your stage is the picture sort or the plastic sort. But in the main this has been at once the pioneer and the most advanced formal permanent stage. Copeau may very well ask his fellow-directors pointedly, "What becomes of *unity* on your stages when the *décor* is changed from act to act?"

Very like the *Vieux Colombier*, inspired by it, and designed with the advice of Louis Jouvet, was that Marais Theatre in Brussels where René Moulaert for a brief season presented a variety of plays in essentially the same architectural scene. Here an existing proscenium remained; but the three-level arrangement of fore-stage and main stage, joined with steps, and balcony, gave the same freedom of movement, concentration of attention and neutrality of background so noticeable at the *Vieux Colombier*. There were also the typical permanent portals; but in this case footlights and proscenium strips largely took the place of the confessed lanterns for lighting.

Of projects for similar stages, a model by Ladislas Medgyes offers the greatest opportunity for varied movement, having four playing levels, with open ramps instead of hidden stairways from main platform to balcony. But here, in an effort to add even more opportunity for the up-and-down movement so valued by directors, a large pit occupies the center of the main stage—the very space, it seems to me, that should be the most carefully cleared and guarded spot of the whole composition. In other words, here is a formal stage which, instead of thrusting the action up and forward, leaves out almost entirely the stage center, the *treteau* itself.

A project by Alexander Bakshy—chief proponent, among writers in English, of the presentational as against the representational performance—arranges movable stages on two levels above the main stage floor; and the three platforms are flanked by constructions that apparently bring the balcony floor forward at the sides almost to the stage front, with two breaks in level. This design affords a remarkable sense of enclosure and intimacy for the main playing space—a great asset—but there is no indication how the problems of lighting are to be met.

All of these permanent stages are reminiscent of the English Elizabethan theatre, and most of the artists who have developed them would acknowledge a debt to William Poel, who did so much to establish the facts about Shakespeare's playhouse and to revive the spirit of that time in the staging of old plays. There is no special virtue, of course, in clinging to exact details of the Elizabethan or any other ancient theatre, now when conditions are so different—it is the freedom and expressiveness of the general *form* that we want—but certainly there is special interest in a structure so like the seventeenth-century playhouse as the little Maddermarket Theatre at Norwich, England. It has been called "the first Elizabethan playhouse seen since 1642," but it has modern modifications none the less. Its upstanding, uncurtained stage, with permanent side walls pierced by portals, and permanent rear wall with balcony over a small curtained inner stage, are more than reminiscent of the early sixteen hundreds; but movable walls are set in at times, and extensive use is made of designed curtains, and of modern lighting equipment, to accomplish the variety considered necessary for a repertory drawn from more than twenty centuries of playwriting.

From this first type of architectural stage to the sculptural stages, as developed particularly by Norman-Bel Geddes, is not such a far cry as one might at first glance think. The difference is that the sculptured platform is architecture in the lump, without those stylistic refinements and ornaments which too often are accepted as the all of architecture. Here is the naked stage shaped to afford a series of scenes of diversified character, not in slavish imitation of places in nature, but with a bow to the essential shapes and flavors of those places. I think that Geddes has not so far attempted to design a stage of this sort for permanent use with many plays; he has modeled a new stage for every drama, arranging each time his playing platforms, ramps and suggested walls to accommodate the action as he visualizes it in the rôle of director. There is no logical reason why such a sculptured universal stage cannot be designed and utilized for a wide repertory. One may even feel that Geddes' own productions of *Arabesque*, where comparatively large changes in scene were made (always in view of the audience), and of *Jehanne d'Arc*, which was much more abstract and out of time and place, might be performed on the stage he designed for *The Mother of Christ*, without too great loss to the acting and action values.

These stages are all, of course, without curtains; and all are designed for use with a flexible lighting equipment which will bring into prominence one feature after another of the diversified "structure" in addition to the central downstage playing space. The advantages of this type of stage over the usual changing-picture sort, in economy, in freedom of physical movement, in emphasis on the set-out actors, are enormous. Geddes' project for a production of his arrangement of Dante's *Divine Comedy* is so gigantic in conception, so beyond ordinary means and day-by-day theatre, that it demands only a note here: that its stage is similar to these less extraordinary ones in being sculpturally conceived, wholly plastic, uncurtained, and first of all a place for shaping scenes in light.*

The sculptured stage, of course, being set in space, must be backed by

* Forty designs are reproduced in *A Project for a Theatrical Presentation of the Divine Comedy of Dante Alighieri*, by Norman-Bel Geddes. New York, 1924.

*something*—if the theatre is enclosed, not open-air—bare wall of the stage box or curtains or a specially prepared wall. Under the localized lighting, this background seldom comes into view, and never prominently. For *Jehanne d'Arc* screens were used as backing, for *Arabesque* a neutral curtain, and for *Dante* huge wing-like structures rise out of the stage, with gauze hung behind. The Germans, who also have occasionally exercised their talents in modeling sculptural stages, have the advantage of being able to place the construction within the apparently unlimited space of sky-domes. The outline sketch of Eduard Sturm's project for *Manfred* is typical of experiment in this direction.

Just as the *Dante* project is interesting as a very special rather than a type thing, so certain famous productions like those given by Reinhardt in "circuses," although steps toward formal stage practice, warrant passing mention rather than extensive description. Even *The Miracle* production in New York, although it was set in a theatre, partook of the nature of an individual "stunt" rather than an epoch-making event on the road to the future. Scenically it was very impressive: a stage and part of an auditorium completely built over into apparently an actual cathedral—and where is there a more atmospheric, more glamorous and more usable formal stage than in certain cathedrals? But it was not at the heart of our present problem, which is the permanent stage shaped as continuing decoration.

Out of Reinhardt's circus performances developed that *Grosses Schauspielhaus* in Berlin which was meant to be a type example of gigantic show-house for "people's theatre" productions. Here an apron stage juts well out into the auditorium, "in the midst of the audience"—for Reinhardt had learned the value of an uncurtained, architectural scene in establishing an immediate *rapport* with the audience—and behind that are steps up to a long narrow platform stage. So much of the playing space is open, permanent, and adjustable to different levels, a true architectural stage. Its backing, however, is a curtain in an arch, and behind that is another complete stage, with revolving center and sky-dome. The theatre is thus a compromise, an attempt to combine the elements of the revived formal stage with the contemporary peep-hole stage; and like most such spectacular compromises it is just about half satisfactory to the modernists and less than that to the conservatives. Certain productions in the house have been finely dramatic, and Reinhardt utilized cunningly the advantages afforded by the fore-stage. But in general, the problem of the "theatre of the five thousand," the opportunity for the playhouse that makes the naked stage the altar of a people's cathedral, has yet to find solution.

Reinhardt's productions at Vienna, in the *Redoutensaal*, a theatre constructed in an imperial ballroom, and on temporary platform stages at Salzburg, suggest a harking back to that bare stage used for outdoor productions during the Renaissance, and carried indoors on occasion: a long platform, in effect, not noticeably shaped as was the Elizabethan, not connected with the auditorium floor or an apron, and with curtains or screens as the main accessories.

The *Redoutensaal* theatre has been extravagantly admired by those who see a heightening of some personal conception of "theatricalism" in the regal beauty of the ornamented hall, the patent artificiality and glamour of the crystal chandeliers, the richness of the Gobelin tapestries, and in the general air of formal elegance in the platform backing—bare as is the acting space upon it. And certainly here is one of the most fruitful of contemporary experiments in gaining decorative values from stage and auditorium as one entity, and not from pictures placed successively on the stage. The wall that backs the platform is a curved and ornamental architectural construction in keeping with the richness of the ballroom, but in a more restrained and neutral manner; and it holds doorways for exits and entries, and graceful stairs to a balcony above at the back. On this pleasantly formal stage a mere indication of "scenery" has proved enough: acting has become the chief resource of the directors. By a convention which Meyerhold had already utilized elsewhere, the stage and the audience are lighted by the same chandeliers, another link thus being forged to bind the actor and the spectator in intimacy. It is to be questioned whether a wide variety of plays could be performed here appropriately; the regal, distinctive atmosphere of the place is too heightened. But it is a stage that has shaken itself free from the illusion-fallacy, free from the need for machinery or proscenium or picturing, free for expression within the one limitation imposed by the stylistic ballroom architecture.

A good deal of abstract interest in a special type of semi-formal stage was shown in France in 1925, when the architects Auguste and Gustave Perret and André Granet designed for the temporary Exposition of Decorative Arts a theatre with a "tri-partite" stage. Practically nothing was done to prove the potentialities of the theatre: there was no series of appropriate dramatic productions directed by artists with an understanding of modernism in the theatre. But the stage form stimulated excited if not bitter controversy. The composition included a large removable apron stage over what was at other times the orchestra pit, a main stage divided by permanent structural pillars into a central scene and two lateral scenes, and a back stage arrangement of pillars and plaster wall that at least in part could stand as a permanent decorative background.

As a matter of fact, the architects here were harking back not so much to the truly architectural stages as to the theatre of the "simultaneous scene." What they had in mind was that this Exposition theatre would help solve scenic problems by allowing three scenes to be set at once for successive use, and they made provision for three curtains. But an artist who discounts separate scene-making and regards the design of this stage without its curtains will discover unusual potentialities and a certain resident nobility of form. (Plate 108.)

Before turning from the architectural stage to the consideration of the space stage, I want to add one more word of general theory, or belief. I personally see a value in *structural form* in the carpentered outstanding formal stage which seems to me hurtfully lacking in space and Constructivist stages. Those theatrical values that we talk about so much, that we want to reënforce, intensify and heighten, are very vague things; and I believe that somehow the shaped permanent stage gives them backbone, continuity and solidity. Light in space seems to me too soft a background for continual use: I want this hard lump of stage as a core—and I see a nobility gained from the design of the continuing austere but responsive platform.

Hermann Rosse, experimenter with novel ideas of decoration, and one of the most far-sighted of our theorists, has written somewhere of the "pure structural beauty of an unadorned building, a beautifully finished platform," and foresees "a slow development of the purely constructive stage and the oratory platform to a new type of church-like theatre with reflecting domes, beautiful materials, beautiful people . . ." We cannot build that theatre rightly until after we have explored all that light projected into space can bring us in theatrical expressiveness. But I think that in the end we shall return to the formal stage, in some expressive and sensitive manifestation made possible by the precision and elasticity of typical machine-age materials and inventiveness.

# XIII

## THE SPACE STAGE

THE conception of the physical stage primarily *as space* has a suggestive parallel in modern architecture. Certain of the stage artists and directors insist on getting away from the thought of decorated surfaces surrounding the dramatic action, or even the thought of a permanent constructed visible background, in favor of space sculptured in light to show up and emphasize the actors and action. Just so a whole school of radicals in architecture point to the fallacy of beginning building art with a study of walls and their decoration, and insist upon spatial relationships as the heart of their problem of design. In both cases it is more than a mere matter of space as usually thought of; there is a vague feeling that in certain spatial adjustments there is a living beauty, a fourth-dimensional formal quality. There is an element involved far beyond any contributive beauty to be wrung from shallow surface decoration.

The fundamental thing differentiating the typical space stage from the formal architectural stage is the emphasis on a spot picked out of darkness, a little piece detached from a void, with the consequent suppression of structural surroundings. The director wants no sense of a building, no conscious joining of a stage and an auditorium. Here is a different sort of Expressionism from that of the theorists who would keep the physical theatre forward, who would utilize the constant presence of the stage as one element in reënforcing essential theatricality.

The adherents of the void stage feel that they gain greater values out of unhampered manipulation of lighting as a dramatic medium than any they lose in abandoning architectural decoration and solidity. They even feel that a space stage, freed from carpentered rigidity, is able to capitalize the potentialities of modern lighting equipment and to some extent modern stage machinery in a way far more in keeping with machine-age aesthetics than is possible in any other type of building.

The space stage as known so far is usually the old proscenium-frame picture-box affair cleared out, and wired and equipped for extraordinary light range and control. A horizon-dome may back the stage, in which case the director's problems are measurably simplified. It is obvious that this cleared-out stage can be used not only for the naked spot-out-of-darkness scene, but beyond that for anything from the slightest indication of reality to a fully representative scene, which of course is wholly impossible on a formal stage like Copeau's. It is not the stage itself that determines the modernism of the productions here, but the artist's intent and method in using the stage or the space in it.

I cannot do better than go back and speak of one production that proved for me the potentialities of the picked-out stage. *Masse-Mensch*, as it was produced at the *Volksbühne* in Berlin, began with a scene in which a restricted, undecorated area of action alone was visible, seemingly picked out of a black void by lighting. In this pool of light, down close to the audience, three figures appeared, hands clasped, and began to speak their lines directly, rapidly, almost precipitately—for the play like the settings was Expressionistic, unnatural, out of time and place. The effect was far more emotional, more holding, than anything I can imagine in a picture setting, however simple. There was absolutely nothing to take the attention from the players and their speech and action. Other scenes were played on a darkened stage, sometimes with black curtains surrounding the playing space and sometimes with the immense stage opened up like a cathedral at night before the dead horizon-dome, with larger areas and groups of players picked out by the light. In two scenes there were unobtrusive and undecorative structures like athletic-field "bleachers" hidden in the veil of darkness at the back and at one side; and when these were gradually filled with actors, with the light creeping over to reveal nothing but a sea of faces, the effect was extraordinarily decorative in a sheer dramatic sense. The scene in which the workingmen on the bleachers sang the *Internationale* on this otherwise naked stage, followed by the opening of the curtains opposite for the entry of troops and a volley, remains in my mind as one of the most vivid scenes in all my playgoing experience. The sheerness, the directness, were used here for melodramatic effect; but in other scenes the drama was not mixed with violence, although always far from nature. In one scene huge screen-like shapes towered over the area of light—they might have been meant to suggest cliffs or walls askew, but were more probably designed only for an abstract emotional effectiveness. Again a red cage stood out as if on a black hilltop against a dim sky. Only one scene touched material reality, suggested actual place, when the bases of two architectural columns showed in an opening between curtains. Thus in one play was the gamut run from decoration wholly by light in a void to a detached indication of a natural locale. And that is the range of the space stage as most of the advanced adherents of the idea are using it.

I do not mean that this production illustrated the profounder and more meticulously conceived aspects of drama as made effective through mathematical or musical manipulation of space. One must turn to the later work of Adolphe Appia for a demonstration of the subtler uses of the idea.

Appia, working forward from the postulates of his early writings, the insistence that the actor's presence, his three-dimensional body, must be made to dominate, that right emphasis is impossible in the flat two-dimensional setting, and that light is the living factor to take the place of the old dead sort of scene, came later to a new conception of the values of space and of architectural elements sparingly used. Having entirely discounted the pictorial values of the proscenium stage, he arrived at the belief that the actor would stand out best in space against reticent architectural masses, with flat surfaces and very few accentuated lines or angles. "Living space" became the heart of his physical scene.

Appia's production of *The Tidings Brought to Mary* at Hellerau in 1913 was a landmark in progress toward a new stage. Kenneth Macgowan* wrote: "The stage and the scene were identical and consisted merely of a complex of movable platforms and steps, supplemented by simple flats and hangings. These could be arranged almost endlessly." But this stage was even less simple than the starkly architectural affair Appia has since come to champion; it was, indeed, not unlike the plastic arranged stages with stairs, platforms and pylons dreamed and sketched by Craig in the period when he was working with screens.

Later Appia wrote that all the theatre need be is "an elementary structure

* *The Theatre of Tomorrow*, New York, 1921.

designed simply to give shelter to the space where we work. No scene, no auditorium; merely a room naked and empty—and expectant; everywhere space cleared for the things actually used; a full lighting equipment." And his drawings for scenes, as reproduced in those two remarkable brochures, *l'Oeuvre d'Art Vivant* and *Art Vivant ou Nature Mort?* indicate just such nudity, just such throwing of emphasis on the acting that goes into the scene. A platform placed across the end of a hall, with steps up to it, and perhaps a solid or pierced wall to carry up one line and mass in contrast, or a pillar, each such element being placed with exact attention to the dramatic uses and effects of the lines, proportions, shadows; the floor apparently made of the same materials and blending into the wall or pillar; and at the back as near nothingness as can be achieved. Copeau and Geddes and Reinhardt, for all their confessed stages, have not approached this simplicity, this abstraction, this capitalization of movement in space. It seems the last word in the attempt to heighten the presence of the actor, to subordinate the inanimate elements in the scene, to put the emphasis on living action in living light. It is not in the current of full-blooded Expressionism, perhaps, in that it does not utilize dynamically the physical form of an obvious stage, or the more melodramatic values of lighting; but who shall say that it is not the most *sensitively* expressive stage yet devised since light was conquered and made a major theatric medium? (Plates 112 and 113.)

Of those who have most successfully opened up their stages to unencumbered space and light, consistently erecting thereon barest indications of reality, Leopold Jessner, director of the State Theatre in Berlin, and his designer Emil Pirchan, have been both pioneers and foremost practitioners. They are likely to build their stage out with an apron on a lower level, which has the double advantage of adding to the playing space and giving opportunity for increased movement up and down; and they may have a platform well back on the main stage, or steps (Jessner so noticeably capitalized stairs as playing space that the word "Jessner-treppen" is in every theatre vocabulary in Germany). On this series of levels, alone or with a column or balustrade or arch, Jessner plays his actors in or against the light. When the curtain rises on the performance, one is likely to have the impression of looking into limitless space, with the shaped platform or decorative terrace placed in the brighter light forward to center the action. This platform is probably in itself unobtrusively decorative. It may be carpeted (it was in rose-red throughout in *Don Carlos*), and it may be edged with gold; and it stands against a horizon-dome that is gratefully soft to the eye, velvet dark or impalpably light or opalescent, as may be appropriate. Levels in space, with an intimation of architecture here or the furnishings of a throne room there—such is the summary of Jessner's "stage decoration."

Others carry the intimation of reality one step farther, without losing the sense of detachment from life. A little conglomerate of columns, or windows and doors, or screens, together with the necessary furniture, is formed into a decorative vignette and set out in space. Lee Simonson used the method memorably in the Theatre Guild production of *The Failures*, and even on the small Garrick Theatre stage succeeded in creating the impression of a detached bit of nature, a bit pulled free and set into light in a void stage (plate 115). The method came into prominence first in Germany, as an alternate of painted Expressionism, a different sort of distortion, and there on the domed stages absolute isolation of the lighted vignette was possible. In the Guild Theatre Lee Simonson has occasionally reverted to the principle in a larger way, building a half-realistic sculptural scene and then setting it out as if swimming in toned light. Such was the impression afforded by the settings for Werfel's *The Goat Song*.

This consideration of the "fragmentary setting in space" has led me back as close to selective realism as is proper, perhaps, in a consideration of Expressionistic stages. Let us turn instead to those indications of reality that lead less to realization of place than to Constructivist means for acting. If one takes the trouble to run over the simplified scenes that have been most widely heralded among students of stagecraft during the last ten years, one will find not a few examples that eliminated pretty much everything except playing space and "practicable" elements. These were not strictly and technically Constructivist settings, because the practical elements for successive scenes were not woven into one composition, with consequent discarding of the proscenium curtain. In a sense, Craig's screen settings were designed from a conception of the space stage rather than from a "picturing" point of view; and some of his simplest sketches and models might well be

considered steps in the direction of Constructivism. Apropos of the ideas of Jessner and Appia and the space stage and a very few architectural elements, one remembers Craig's designs for *The Steps*. In the description, after he speaks of "dramas where speech becomes paltry and inadequate," he adds, ". . . among all the dreams that the architect has laid upon the earth, I know of no more lovely things than his flights of steps leading up and leading down, and of this feeling about architecture in my art I have often thought how one could give life (not a voice) to these places, using them to a dramatic end. When this desire came to me I was continually designing dramas wherein the place was architectural and lent itself to my desire. And so I began with a drama called 'The Steps.' "

Robert Edmond Jones even some ten years ago made sketches for a production of Maeterlinck's *The Seven Princesses* which foreshadowed Constructivism in its use of skeleton architecture set in space: an outline of a Gothic apse on a semi-circular stair unit, lighted out of darkness. One recalls also that many of the individual scenes in that well-remembered if unsuccessful production of *Macbeth* in New York, under the direction of Arthur Hopkins and in settings by Jones, had this same naked quality. The production failed of its chief purpose because the acting had no relation to the settings, although planned to be similarly expressive. But throughout the scenes there was a sense of visual abstract dramatic form, derived out of a personal emotional reading of the poet's text; they were not real or suggestive of detailed reality, and they were not symbolic in the shallow sense; they were directly expressive of dramatic feeling, in terms of light, color and a very few more or less architectural constructions set out in a void—a formal and theatrical equivalent of some vaguely remembered necessary actuality.

The same dependence upon line and abstract composition, equally far from actuality, is illustrated in the two scenes from Alexander Tairoff's production of *Phèdre* at the Kamerny Theatre in Moscow (plate 114). Movement plays so great a part in Tairoff's presentations, be it noted, that his school of the theatre has special courses in juggling and acrobatics; and one of his fundamental requirements is "an exact working out of the stage levels: these must be built differently for every play, they must be built according to the dynamic and rhythmic-plastic requirements of the play and are used as a piano for revealing the actor's movements and emotions." It is easy to see how this theory, with Tairoff as with Meyerhold, later developed into full-blown Constructivism. At this period, composition in planes on a naked stage had become a source of extraordinary dramatic effectiveness. In the *Phèdre* production it was a case of planes used for movement's sake, with the edges emphasized as abstract decorative line. The "directions" of the composition underlined the action of the players, and the total design reënforced the director's conception of the play.

There is, however, this one great difference between the work of Jones, Appia, Jessner, and Tairoff in his early days, and the work of the avowed Constructivists: the latter insist not only that the two-dimensional decorative elements must be discarded, but that the stage construction must be designed *anti-decoratively*.

To many of us it has seemed that the great merit of Craig, Appia, Copeau, Geddes, Jones, Jessner and their fellows lies in the finding of a new decorativeness to take the place of the flat picture sort, a decorativeness more appropriately theatrical in being three-dimensional and resolved out of the typically stage mediums of light, space and architecture. In denying the validity of *any* visual decorative values, in affirming that aesthetic intent in the arranging of the stage can only harm the action thereon, the Constructivists have uttered a revolutionary cry more radical and more far-reaching in its implications than any other in the whole history of staging.

# XIV

## CONSTRUCTIVISM

THE typical Constructivist setting may be described as a skeleton structure made up of the physically necessary means for acting a play: an agglomeration of the stairs, platforms, runways, etc., called for by the dramatist, stripped to their basic and structural forms, held together by plain scaffolding, and arranged to permit the running off of the play at its fullest theatrical intensity. It is all the scenes of a play simplified to the bone and woven into one scene. Always the true Constructivist setting is conceived for use without a curtain and to stand in space from the time the audience arrives until it leaves. It is utterly (and finely) unnatural, in its grouping together of many elements detached from life, and in its bareness, its lack of every casual detail of nature and of such usual elements as walls and ceilings. Every plank and post of it is tested by the rigid question of its functional use. It is the "practicables" of the old pictorial scene plucked out of the picture, skeletonized and nailed together for safe usage. What "design" is expended on weaving these naked structural things into one whole theoretically has the sole purpose of capitalizing movement as a revealing theatrical element.

One example may look like a mere scaffolding holding up three or four platforms, some probably tilted, at various levels, with stairs or ladders or runways between and from the stage floor. Another may be far more involved, with platforms railed, wheels added, cages, awnings, benches, bridges, lattices, window frames, mere "shapes." Where one is delicate and intricate, almost lace-like in effect, another will be composed of heavy masses, broad ramps instead of ladders, blocks instead of posts. In some there is very obvious attempt to achieve a machine-like combination of heaviness and precision. In them all, from the auditorium standpoint, the spectator "sees the works." Movement of the construction itself, or of its parts, is added as an effect in extreme cases.

Despite protestations that nothing beyond functional use determines the construction, the spectator may occasionally make out a complete balcony here or a sheltering corner of a room there, a recognizable bit from ordinary life. But it is true that the Constructivists of the far Left look on practitioners like Rabinovitch, with his famous skeleton colonnade for *Lysistrata* (plate 119), as a compromiser of the principles of the true faith. He has even been accused of romanticising. Because his naked columns were joined at the top and bottom by pieces reminiscently curved, he had betrayed the mother that begat him.

What are the sources of this impatience with anything not strictly utilitarian? It is, as a matter of fact, part and parcel of a revolutionary creed that has stirred up bitter dissension in the fields of all the arts during the last decade, from literature to architecture. It is born of the laudable desire to rid art of excessive ornament, sentiment and high polish, characteristics of the weak nineteenth century. If we get not back to structure, naked emotion and expressive form as the bases of art creation, we might just as well resign ourselves to the continuing weak echoes of stylistic art that have persisted from Victorianism and before: with sentimental story-telling, with a photographically realistic theatre, with pretty reproductive and anecdotal painting, with architecture in watered imitation of the great outworn styles. The revolution in its various phases dates back as far as Cezanne in painting, abandoning everything else in the search for a realization of "form," to Louis Sullivan in architecture, going back to honest uncompromising structure, to the Expressionist impulse in all the arts. But chiefly it was the engineer and the designer of machines who inspired the "utilitarian" wing of the modernist army. Particularly, the American skyscraper, in its nudity and daring, is cited as opening the eyes of the young European radicals to a new and different sort of beauty—not the skyscrapers as our average overcultured architects left them in the end, with weakly decorative and inappropriate façades hung on, but in their unfinished skeleton state or as a rare genius like Sullivan left them.

Beyond that was the inspiration out of machinery. I can speak wholeheartedly with these radicals here. I think that no other creative artists in America to-day are quite so worthy of praise and recognition as those who have made our automobiles—absolutely expressive of their purpose, true to machine materials of the age, beautiful to the eye without an added line of ornament. This directness, this truth, this sheerness, this expressive beauty, was what we needed to get back to in our "fine" arts. The Dadaists wanted to begin by destroying everything that had come down to the present as an art heritage from the past. They wanted to sweep out clean. They saw no way out but to blast into eternity everything accumulated in the name of art. Steadier heads (I think!) understood that much of the art of the past had been absolutely right for its eras; foresaw that an opportunity to promenade in the spirit of those eras might occasionally refresh the spirit of man; that we were simply wrong to hold to the frills and echoes of other times in a period of new machine-age standards. The machine, with its massiveness and its intricacy, its rightness, its perfect functioning, its precise shaping and its clean surfaces, its balance—this was a clue to an art for the times. Here Constructivism began.

Most of us who are interested particularly in the theatre forget that Constructivism came into art, as a word and as a mode, not in connection with the stage but as an attempt at an independent studio form of creative expression. The Russian Constructivists designed models out of machine materials, steel, armor-plate, glass, copper, wood, wire, wheels, springs; and these they exhibited along with Cubist pictures and sculptures.

It is possible that the thing came into the playhouse as a separate theatrical development. One can argue that the steady march of stage decoration toward greater and greater simplicity, and finally toward elimination, made the purely functional stage a logical and inevitable outcome. Decoration as such dropping away, left bare structure. But it seems to me far more likely that theatre directors, studying the independent constructions, said to themselves, "What wonderful things to act upon!"; and straightway the Constructivists were called in to serve the theatre—the theatre in which movement had recently become such a resource.

Meyerhold is generally credited with originating the mode on the stage, with Tairoff close after him. Jakouloff and Popova are usually named as the most important early practitioners. They brought into being the skeleton setting designed to serve as the physical stage on which every act of a given play could be performed. Whatever the origin, it was a fitting climax to the simplifying-eliminating process to which stage decoration had been submitted during a quarter of a century previous.

If a stage setting can be thus designed, or put together, as logically, with as much truth to purpose, with as perfect feeling for the right usable material, as in the making of machines, why is it not the perfect utilitarian scene? And if it is perfect in the utilitarian way, can it avoid then being decorative in the broader sense? I for one believe that if it achieves perfection as a machine for theatric action, it will necessarily be decorative. As long as man designs the machine with a feeling for thorough workmanship, for the final "rightness" of the mechanism in its job, he cannot but add that formal quality that gives it an aesthetic appeal, that marks it at the same time as art.

The avowed anti-decorationists not only claim that it is necessary to strip the setting of every shred of decorative appeal, but assert that the creation of art can come only by absolute design-for-use without the slightest admixture of so-called aesthetic intention. There is an arbitrary attempt here to limit aestheticism to self-conscious manipulation of "fine arts" materials. But art, I believe, may arrive where there is consciously or unconsciously the desire to create the thing not only usably but with clean-cut thorough workmanship and with a mark of its absolute rightness on it. The decorative value resides in that right form.

The anti-decorationists seem to me right just half the way along the line—to this extent: the aesthetic appeal is more direct, fresher, more basic, if the decorative quality is achieved instinctively, while the artist is apparently absorbed wholly in the problems of use, than when he tries to add to the essential thing through a mode of ornament or a formula for composition or decoration. They are right in revolting against too much manufacture of art by theory, too much academism, too much acceptance of surface decoration as art, too much love of technical polish, too much shallow stylistic pretense. But for all the rightness of the desire to prick the balloon of pretension and dogma flown by accepted art authorities, they cannot separate art expression even in the machine from a legitimate decorativeness. Unless they are perversely unworkmanlike, they cannot, being artists and creators at heart, make a thing that is noticeably undecorative. It seems to me that they *are* thus perverse when they set their construction against an old stage wall without covering its obviously inappropriate inscriptions, radiators and sprinkler systems. They can utilize bareness, sheerness of surface, beautifully; but carelessness and shoddy workmanship and perverse loose ends are no virtue in the machine age.

So, not believing that the true Constructivist setting can be anti-decorative —only that it is decorative *in its own different way*—I find the mode one of the most logical of the several devised to take the place of the pictorial scene. It affords wonderful freedom of action, its nudity is a virtue in the greater opportunity afforded for spatial composition, and it solves as well as the formal stage the problem of running off many-scened plays without interruption (but only for one play). Personally I still see a flat uninvolved architectural backing as the best means of setting out the quieter forms of action, and I feel the need for a solid permanent architectural central platform for acting as the basis for my composition or construction. Moreover, I distrust intricacy of structure as likely to distract almost as much as a picture. But I think any designer of a stage or settings would be a fool if he did not learn from the Constructivist something of variety, pliability, economy, truth to use. The lesson might well be called to the attention of playwrights also.

The moving settings still seem to me wholly impossible for the vast majority of plays in which we are here interested, where the acted drama is the first consideration. That is not to say that a special form of theatrical entertainment may not evolve around them. S. Margoline, writing recently in the *Little Review*, evidently saw movement of the setting itself as a prime characteristic of Constructivism: "Everything comes as a surprise in this new kind of 'construction.' To accompany a crescendo in the play, the stage or the objects begin to turn and to metamorphose. Architects and engineers are superceding the painter. The theatre looks like a kind of factory. The actor is merely a laborer in the 'theatre shop.' He produces a certain number of values. He is no longer a player, he works." But that is getting over into the field of the glorification of the mechanical at the expense of traditional *acted* drama, the field of Kiesler and Prampolini, which we have already ruled out of the present discussion.

Those first Constructivist settings that were published to the world out of Russia a few years ago now seem a little self-consciously nude, stiff and self-proclaimingly stripped of all softening human influences. But later even in Meyerhold's theatres they have appeared to be more instinctively designed to add their own contributive bit to the interest of the unfolding drama even while serving it practically, to live with it rather than merely to offer enlivening opportunity for agile feet.

In Tairoff's Kamerny Theatre, in the Jewish Habima Theatre in Moscow, in the Musical Studios of the Moscow Art Theatre, Constructivism in various phases has been developed to a recognized and recognizable mode; and of course all over Germany the principle is being tried out. My illustrations (plates 118 to 121) are chosen to show the variety of its manifestations, but the persistence of its utilitarian idea.

In final summary: The story of stage decoration extends over century after century of production on purely architectural stages. It is only in the last tenth of the known history of the theatre that the picture mode of setting has been in existence, that the painter and his materials have held sway on the stages of the Western world. But no art ever capitulated to a new form of exterior dress more completely. For two and a half centuries previous to 1890 the rule of the perspective-painting scenic artist was absolute and unchallenged.

The change in the last thirty-five years has been enormous: a true revolutionary overturn. At first the picture in the proscenium-frame box was altered from a painter's display of virtuosity to a photographically true portrayal of places, in the interest of naturalism. Painted perspective and painted illusion of things disappeared, and plastic elements crept into the scene. The next minor revolution initiated the movement toward simplification which has continued ever since. At first the picture was merely stripped of unnecessary detail. Then suggestion was added to simplification: the picture intimated more than it stated. Then design came in, consciously, and the wholly tasteful simple setting evolved. And as a final improvement in the picture mode, stylization was accomplished, austere or lavish, posteresque or reticent, historical or aesthetic.

It is in this field of thoroughly stylized simple picture scenes that the great mass of fairly progressive directors and decorators practice to-day.

That is, they dress their productions prettily, tastefully, appealingly, with the unifying glamour of a creative stylization over all the places, capitalizing the allurements of color and the subtleties of light, and grasping not a little of the values inherent in abstract composition in line and mass. But they never violate reality beyond the limits set by the selective painters or the "art" photographers. They limit themselves to a selective representation of natural places, an atmospheric approximation of realism.

Beyond them the true experimenters, including, no doubt, the giant figures of to-morrow's theatre, have pursued the ideas of simplification, the plastic and abstraction to the logical conclusion. They have done away with the picture. Accepting as axiomatic that the actor is the all-important element in production, they have acted upon the truth that only a three-dimensional stage can be appropriate to the actor in the round. Simplification led to the elimination of the picture elements, while further study of abstraction and of that typically modern theatric element, living light, led to a new conception of the stage as architecture and space. Being truly Expressionistic, they evolved means of using creatively the physical features of the stage itself and the formal values of space and light. They came in practice to those three types of non-pictorial staging to which I have devoted the final section of my essay: the formal permanent architectural stage (or its cousin, the sculptured stage), the void or emphasized-space scene, and the Constructivist engineered setting.

I see the dramatist now freed from the cramping limitations of realism (unless he feels that he must write unreservedly for the so-called commercial theatre), and I believe that these types of stage are the logical places for acting his new drama, and for all drama written outside the confined realistic era—as far as we can see now. It seems to me that a different formal stage may evolve which, without being a compromise of the underlying principles of modernism, will unite principles out of the three types: a *basic* permanent platform and neutral background, wide and unhampered working and lighting space, and means for constructing easily and quickly when needed the platforms on different levels and the barest intimations of locality that Constructivism affords.

If I personally find in these types of stage the true modernism, and if my reader on the other hand clings to the known virtues of the recognizable picture of a place as setting, neither one of us need be too impatient of the other's viewpoint. Perhaps we both are right, considering the type of play to which we pin our faith and hope. Then too there is a middle ground on which we can meet quite happily if not entirely without suspicion, the field wherein are working those who have kept up with modernist thought, but who modify their radicalism to meet reasonable conditions, conditions that demand that the stage setting have a safe anchor in actual place but without cramping all artistic purpose. Wanting to recognize that there is an evolutionary process still at work in the larger theatre, as well as a revolutionary accomplishment in the exceptional insurgent theatre, and not being really arbitrary at heart, I am choosing my final illustrations from that middle ground: the "flat" setting by Jouvet for *Dr. Knock,* showing how he is working on a picture stage but obviously with the space idea (he says he never designs a setting, only diagrams it); a scene by Robert Edmond Jones as he works on a Broadway stage with Arthur Hopkins; two things by Lee Simonson of the Theatre Guild, setting his realistic scenes, more sculptured than pictured, out in space; and settings by Emil Pirchan, simplifying down the walls of his ceilingless rooms until, without too far violating actuality, he touches so close to abstraction that there is no finding any dividing line between this and Expressionism. These and the works of a goodly number of designers and directors in thorough-going Germany, and in not a few half-experimental American theatres like the Neighborhood Playhouse in New York and the far Western community theatres—these are perhaps the best proof of the march toward a simple formalism, a better indication for the average reader than are the stark accomplishments of the discoverers and prophets.

When we again have great plays, not limited to the peep-hole view of individual lives, the noble plays that we now need far more than any additional changes in stage decoration, and when we have again, as a common thing, noble acting, we shall without question have a thoroughly expressive and appropriate stage ready. For we have found the ways to utilize space, light, levels for movement, and, I think or hope, something out of architecture.

# PART II

## A PICTORIAL RECORD OF STAGE FORMS AND DECORATION FROM THE BEGINNINGS TO 1900

*Plate* 1 These vase drawings represent the earliest known evidence regarding stage forms and decoration, throwing light on a rudimentary type of popular comedy stage of which no actual traces and no adequate descriptions survive: a simple platform for acting, joined by steps with the orchestra below. The Greek theatre as the world knows it from existing ruins, the theatre of the great tragedy-writers, grew rather out of some such "pre-theatre" as is indicated in the conjectural sketch below: a circle for dancing, a hollowed hillside for the spectators, and—since the drama first developed out of processionals and rites in honor of Dionysus—probably a temple in the background.

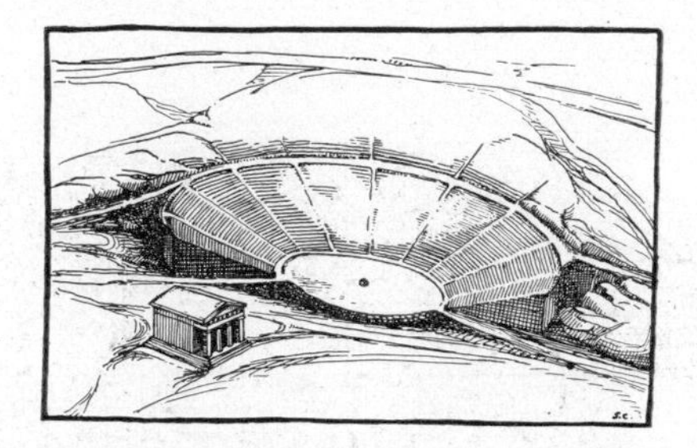

*Plate 2* At the edge of the ever-present dancing-circle of the Greek theatre, a hut or *skene* for the actor was set up, and this gradually was elaborated into a low scene-building, possibly influenced decoratively by the form of the temple. The drawing (above) after a reconstruction by Professor James Turney Allen is probably the nearest approximation we have—though still half conjectural—of the "decoration" before which the plays of Aeschylus, Sophocles and Euripides were first acted, in the Theatre of Dionysus at Athens. The lower drawing, by A. von Gerkan, is a reconstruction of a later scene-building, at Priene. The sketch on this page is a suggested reconstruction of the early Athens theatre by Dörpfeld, the German scholar who directed the thorough excavation of the Theatre of Dionysus, advancing the now generally accepted theory that the truly Greek theatres had no *raised* stages.

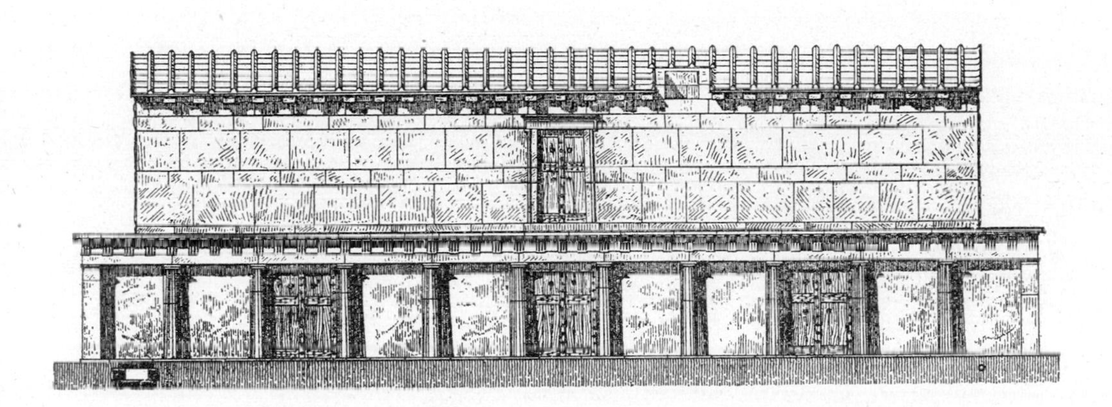

*Plate* 3 Two views of the Fourth Century Theatre of Dionysus, as reconstructed by August Frickenhaus. A conjectural if not hazardous reconstruction of the *skene*, but suggestive here because indicating the relationship of the playing area to the auditorium, the larger "theatre form." The outline sketch below is a reconstruction by E. R. Fiechter of the theatre at Oropus.

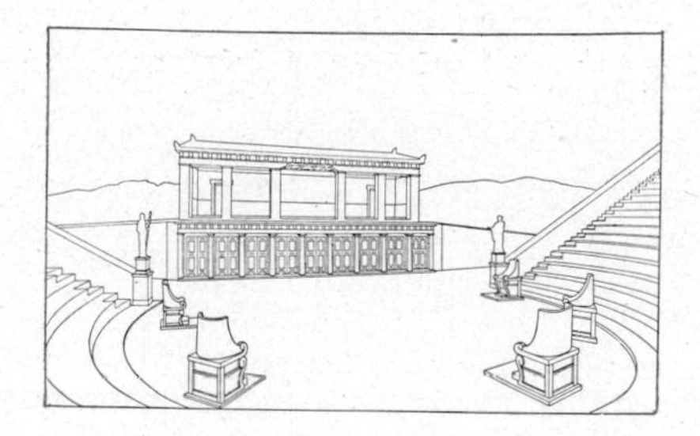

*Plate* 4 Fiechter's sketch of the late Greek theatre at Ephesus. What had been theretofore a *proskenion* construction backing the actor, became a platform stage in the late Greek or Greek-Roman period. Below, an outline sketch by Fiechter of the same theatre.

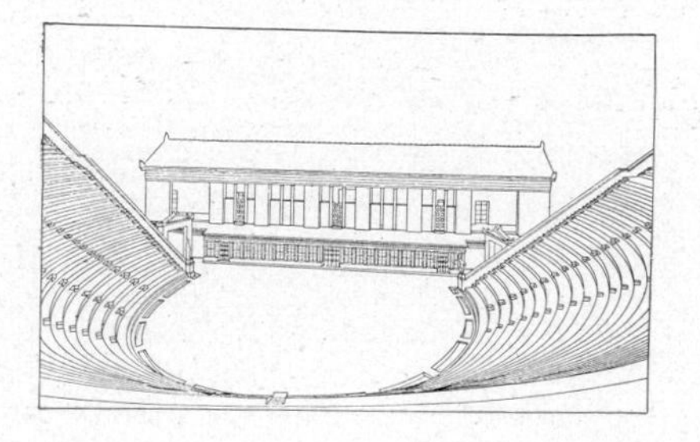

*Plate 5* A drawing of the theatre at Priene, showing the later stage-building, by A. von Gerkan; and a photograph illustrating the state of the theatre to-day, with portions reassembled from the ruins. Below is a sketch of the theatre as it looked from the outside, in which the reader should note the general openness of the structure, and the relative size of the stage-building and the auditorium.

*Plate* 6 Two reconstructions of the stage of the Roman theatre at Orange: above, Caristie's version, from painstaking measurements and study; below, a sketch made under the direction of Camille Saint-Saëns. The full orchestra circle of the Greek theatre has been cut to half and joined to the seating space; all the acting is done on the low stage, now backed with a monumental wall with story upon story of architectural decoration. On this page, a drawing of a bas-relief showing Roman actors against a stage wall.

*Plate 7* The Roman theatre at Aspendus: a reconstruction by Lanckoronski, and a nineteenth-century view of the ruins. On this page, a sketch of the Greek-Roman theatre at Termessus. These views of existing ruins leave no doubt that the world knows the true type-form of the Roman theatre structure, and the manner of architectural decoration of the wall that formed a background to the actors.

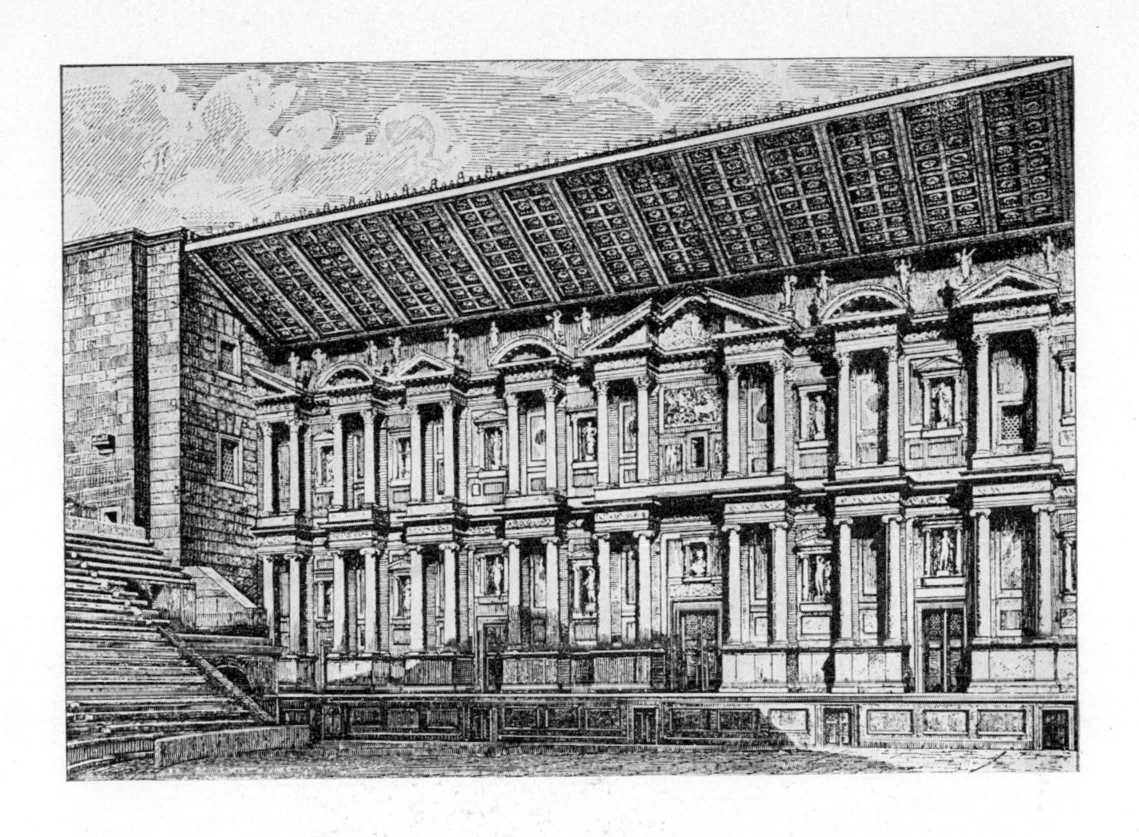

*Plate* 8 Pompey's Theatre in Rome (above): a more or less conjectural restoration by A. Streit, but suggestive of the typical sense of enclosure and richness of ornamentation. The bit of painted screen at the end of the stage is not based on actual evidence. It is known beyond dispute that the Romans utilized clever stage machinery for effects in their spectacles, but there is no contemporary description of painted scenery, although machines for *indicating* change of scene, the *periacti,* had three painted faces. The lower drawing shows a Roman stage wall reconstructed after the evidence of mural paintings preserved at Pompeii, by G. von Cube.

*Plate 9* In direct line between the ancient theatre and the playhouse of to-day is this Italian theatre of the sixteenth century: the Olympic Theatre, or Palladian Theatre, at Vicenza. Suggesting a small Roman theatre roofed over, it has structurally and decoratively most of the features of the late Roman playhouse. But beyond the stage doorways were added, in 1585, the vistas in diminishing perspective, the make-believe architecture that is clearly a forerunner of picture scenery, as seen in the lower photograph opposite. On this page is a drawing after a project of Inigo Jones, indicating that even a traveling English architect was immediately struck by the possibilities of widening one of the doorways and adding the space within the vista to the playing stage.

*Plate* 10 Early in the seventeenth century this first "modern" theatre was built: the Farnese Theatre in Parma. (From a drawing by J. M. Olbrich made for Streit's *Das Theater*.) For the first time the curtained stage is seen in a permanent theatre-building: the stage has been pushed through the doorway, which now becomes the proscenium frame for a picture scene. Below are added sketch plans of type theatres from Greek to Renaissance. Having vaulted over important developments in the history of decoration as such, in order to keep clear the progression of the theatre form from Greek dancing-circle to framed and curtained stage, we shall now go back to trace the origins of the picture elements that are to go within the frame.

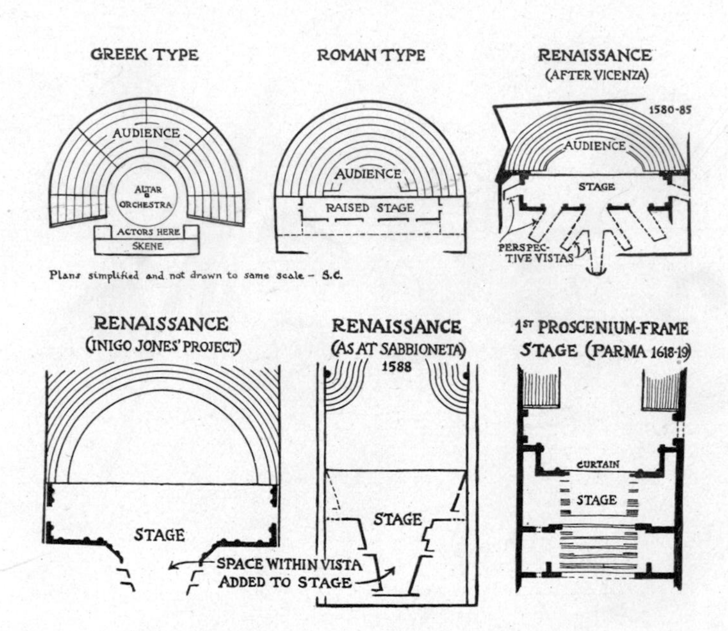

*Plate* 11 After the obscuring of the theatre in the Dark Ages, and long before the building of the revived classic playhouses of the Renaissance, the drama was reborn in the Christian church. Incidents were acted out in the altar area—as magnificent a formal stage as any ever invented. Then the porch outside the church was utilized as a stage. Opposite are shown a typical altar area and a church porch. Below is a sketch by Viollet-le-Duc of a ceremony in Notre Dame de Paris in the eighteenth century.

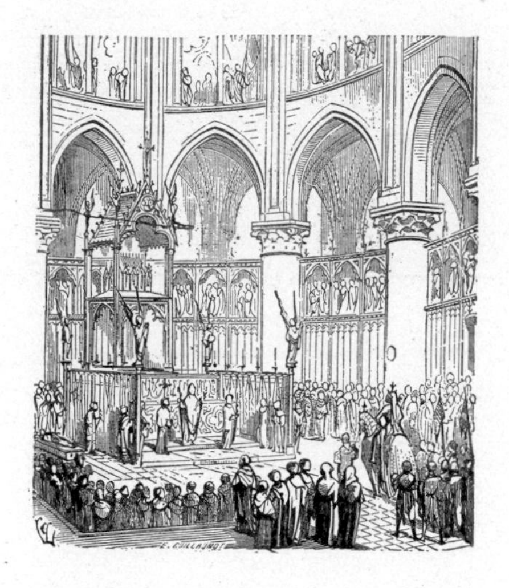

*Plate* 13 The stage of the Valenciennes Passion Play of 1547, after a contemporary miniature by Cailleau. The "stations" or "mansions" are a characteristic feature, with Heaven at the right end of the stage, and a realistic-fantastic "Hell-mouth" at the other. Sometimes termed the "stage of the simultaneous scene."

*Plate* 14 In England particularly the wagon-stage was a common feature of the presentation of the perambulatory Miracle Plays. The cars varied greatly in form, appointments and decorativeness. These are examples of the less elaborate types. The one opposite is from an old engraving (taken from Sharp's *Coventry Mysteries*), and the other, below, from a drawing by Hermann Rosse.

*Plate* 15 An isolated form of stage, not directly connected with the ancient playhouse or with later developments, existed in the theatres wherein the Roman comedies were revived during the fourteenth and fifteenth centuries. This view of a complete theatre is from an illustration in the Trechsel edition of Terence, 1493. Below, a cut of the formal architecture-and-curtains stage, from the same book.

Proscoenium
ædiles
Theatrum
Fornices

*Plate* 16 Examples of plain platform stages, with curtain backgrounds, common in the period when the secular drama was again finding itself, in the sixteenth and seventeenth centuries. Opposite, the reproduction above is after the famous print by Bosse of the stage of Tabarin in Paris; below, an etching by Callot of a stage of the *Commedia dell' Arte* players. On this page a German stage for a folk-play of the Hans Sachs period (1574).

Le monde n'est que tromperie
ou du moins charlatanerie
Comme TABARIN son chapeau
chacun ioue son personnage
tel se pense plus que luy saige
qui est plus que luy charlatan
Messieurs Dieu vous donne bon

Lucia mia.
Bernoualla
Che buona mi

*Plate* 17 The Elizabethan stage in England, after a contemporary drawing of the Swan Theatre by Johann deWitt, 1596. The evidence on which is based a considerable part of to-day's knowledge of the form of Shakespeare's playhouse, with a half-covered, projecting architectural stage. Below are other bits of evidence, from the title-pages of *Roxana* (1632) and *Messallina* (1640). The curtained inner stage, though absent in deWitt's drawing, is generally accepted as a typical feature; although there is as yet no painted "scenery."

tectum
porticus
sedilia
orchestra
mimorum
ædes.
ingressus
proscænium.
Planities sive arena.
Ex observationibus Londinensibus
Johannis de witt

*Plate* 18 Reconstruction of a typical Shakespearean stage by Victor E. Albright. Below is a redrawing of the frontispiece of Kirkman's *Wits* (1672 or 1673).

*Plate* 19 Reconstruction of the Fortune Theatre by Walter H. Godfrey. Below is a reconstruction by G. P. Fauconnet.

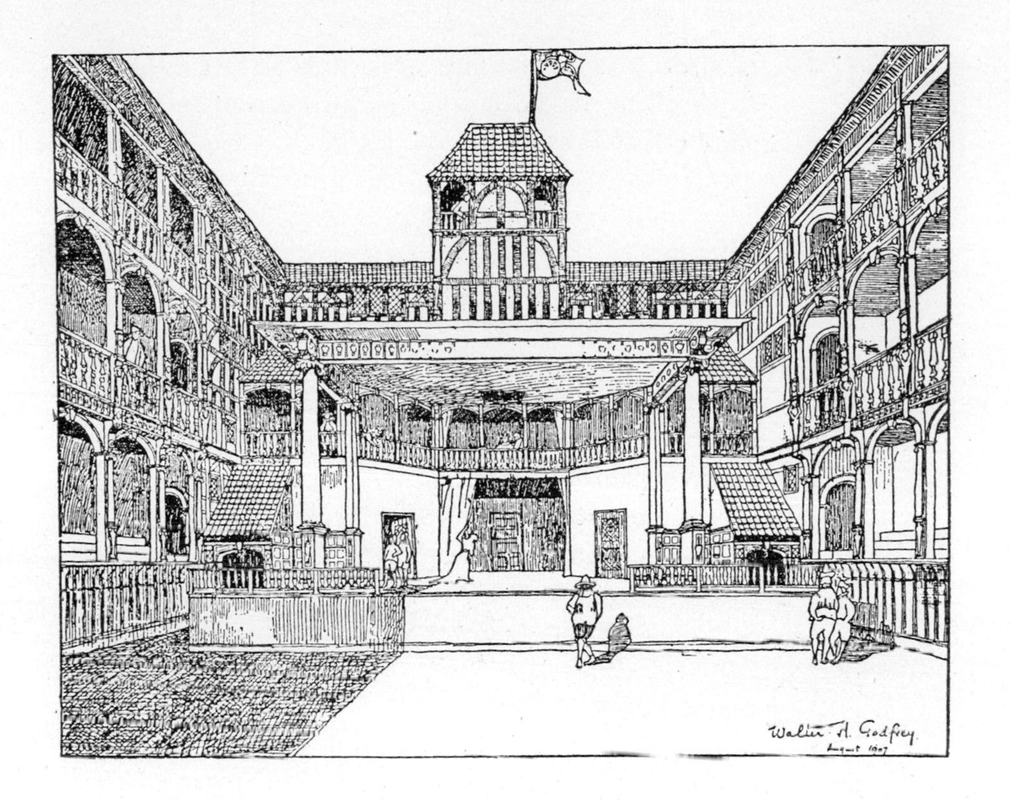
Walter H. Godfrey
August 1907

*Plate* 20 If there is any evidence of a link between the Elizabethan playhouse and the proscenium-frame theatre that is shortly to be introduced to all the countries of Europe, this curious Amsterdam playhouse must be considered to provide it in most generous measure. The architectural stage, so reminiscent of the "stations," with its restricted glimpses of "perspectives" through two apertures at the back, and its main curtain only a few feet back from the platform edge, exhibits features from widely separated forms of theatre (1638). Below are two engravings of outdoor stages more like the Elizabethan type: at left, the Rederijker stage at Ghent (1539), and at right, the Rederijker stage at Antwerp (1561).

DE SCHOUBURGH van binnen
*Op 't Tooneel aen te sien*

*Plate* 21 Transitional stages: the "station stage" plan of the Mysteries applied to secular production, before arrival at the single-scene picture stage. Above, a sketch for a production at Cologne in 1581. Below, a sketch for a multiple scene at the Hotel de Bourgogne, Paris, for *la Folie de Clidamant,* about 1633. The description as put down by Mahelot, the designer, reads: "There must be in the middle of the stage a beautiful palace; and at one side a sea, on which appears a ship rigged with masts and sails, whereon a woman appears and throws herself into the sea; and at the other side a pretty room which opens and closes, where there is a bed made up with sheets. . . ."

While we are here still in the period of the curtainless stage, we have arrived obviously at certain picture elements, evolved partly out of the religious productions and partly out of the first knowledge of the "Italian style." Having examined the several sorts of formal stage from which the picture was wholly absent, or on which its first elements appear, we may now turn back to that first Italian proscenium-frame theatre, and inquire what were the sources in Italy of the imitational setting that was thenceforth to take possession of all European theatres.

CARCER

*Plate* 22 The imitational setting progressed in two main currents: the first had to do with perspectives constructed of make-believe architecture in relief; the second was the progression toward the wholly painted scene. The currents later joined, as we shall see. But taking up the perspective setting first, we find in these cuts from a book by Sebastiano Serlio, 1545, one of the earliest pictorial records of full-stage perspective scenes. He may have evolved them out of a misreading of Vitruvius, who had described such scenes as painted in miniature on the small *periacti*, or he may have drawn them more or less from current practice. Serlio directs that everything except the far end of the vista shall be built out in relief, but with the buildings becoming smaller according as they are farther upstage. The drawing above is the "tragic scene," below, the "comic scene." On this page is a miniature street scene from the Venetian 1586 edition of Terence.

RVFIA

*Plate* 23 The perspective scene with the painted backcloth taking larger place: a setting for the opera *l'Erinto* as given in Munich in 1661 (above); and a design by the German Fuerttenbach, who copied the Italian style in books he published in 1628 and 1640. On this page is a miniature reproduction of a setting for *Il Granchio*, as illustrated in the published play, 1566.

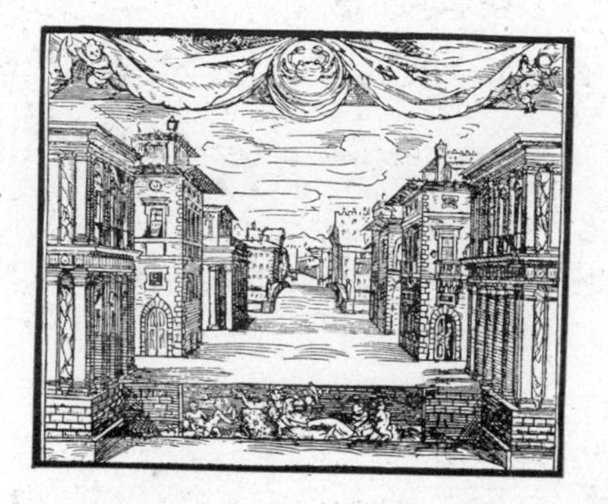

Riti
Iacob Custodi Sculp

*Plate* 24 The perspective scene in France. From the painting in the Museum of the Comédie Française, entitled "*Farceurs François et Italiens . . . Théâtre Royal.*" 1670. There is information here, too, for the student of the history of stage lighting.

Jodelet
Turlupin
Le Capitan Matamore
Gros Guillaume.
Gaultier Garguille
Philippin
polichinelle
Pantalon
Briguelle

*Plate* 25 The glorified perspective scene. To complete the view of the development of the perspective scene, it is necessary to strike ahead of our story chronologically, to show the intricate elaboration of perspectives under the famous Bibienas. The upper picture opposite is after a design by Guiseppe Galli-Bibiena for a dramatic festival at the Court of Bavaria, 1740. The lower is a sketch which is attributed to Giovanni Maria Galli-Bibiena, and illustrates the variety afforded by running the vistas off at angles instead of straight ahead. There were at least half a dozen scene designers in the famous Galli-Bibiena family of Italy, and they begat hundreds of these designs, on and off stages; and straightway their imitators multiplied the hundreds into thousands. Meanwhile the drama was all but perishing, trying to find its way out from among the mazelike pillars and recesses, trying to keep in sight despite the blanket of ornateness. Below is another Bibiena; and a page back will be found a miniature of one of Servandoni's adaptations of the style in France.

*Plate* 26 The main source of the actual painted picture scene lies in the spectacles and theatrical festivals that Italy so loved in Renaissance times. We may even go back to the processions and street pageantry for the earliest suggestion of "painty" stage decoration. In these floats for an "entry," so beautifully etched by Callot, there is much that was later absorbed into the picture setting on the proscenium stage.

Entreé de son Altesse
representant le Soleil
Iac. Callot in. et Fe. Nancy

*Plate* 27 The spectacle elements brought indoors to dress a dramatic production. The setting for the *Ballet de la Royne*, as danced in 1581; after a contemporary print.

*Plate* 28 The non-architectural scene pushed into a frame. An Italian court masque of the Medici, as seen by Callot in the early seventeenth century.

*Plate* 29 The picture scene in the frame. A reëngraving by Huyot from Silvestre's print (1673) of the representation of *la Princesse d'Elide* at Versailles, 1664. Below, a scene from *l'Hypocondriaque,* 1628.

Seconde Journée
Theatre fait dans la mesme allée ſur lequel la Comédye, et le Ballet
de la Princesse d'Elide furent representéz

*Plate* 30 The painter providing elaborate pictures and the machinist devising startling effects worked hand in hand during the seventeenth and eighteenth centuries. This plate illustrates diagrammatically how some of the trick effects were made possible through elaborate stage machinery. Below is a miniature cut of a scene from *les Noces de Thétis et Pélée,* Paris, 1689, with figures floating on clouds, a harbor, ships, and other features popular in the period of glorified spectacle and machine-effects. While these elements developed more properly in opera and masque, they soon overran the stage of the spoken play.

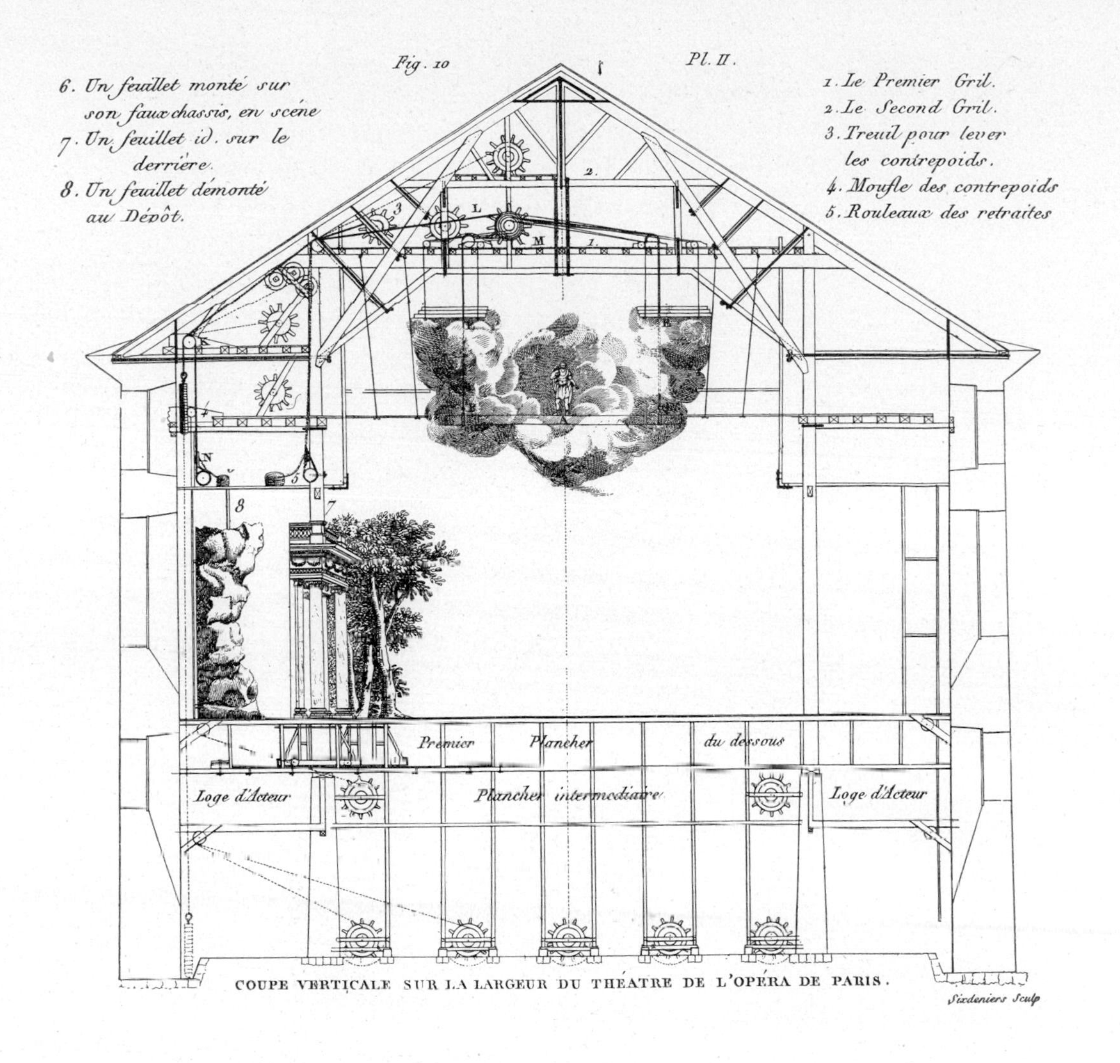


COUPE VERTICALE SUR LA LARGEUR DU THÉATRE DE L'OPÉRA DE PARIS.

*Plate* 31 The typical painter's scene in England. Inigo Jones, having traveled in Italy, introduced the picture mode of scenic design into the private theatres in London. A drawing of a court masque, *Floriméne,* which he staged in 1635, after having passed through periods of experiment with many kinds of set and movable scenery, perspectives, landscapes, machinery, etc. It was not until after the Restoration, however, that picture settings were introduced into the public theatres in London. Below is the third of Serlio's scenes, called the "satyric"—obviously an influence on Jones here, even after ninety years.

*Plate* 32 A production of *Acis et Galatée* at the private theatre of Mme. de Pompadour in the palace at Versailles, 1749. No more graphic illustration was ever made of the complete disguising of the platform stage, in the era of the picturized setting—of the complete triumph of painted make-believe backgrounds as against the architectural stage for lifting actors into view. From an engraving by Guilmet after a contemporary *gouache* by Cochin.

*Plate* 33 Two illustrations of the painter's setting in the picture frame: above, a production in the theatre that later became the home of the *Comédie Française*, 1789; below, the Ventadour (Italian) Theatre in Paris, 1843.

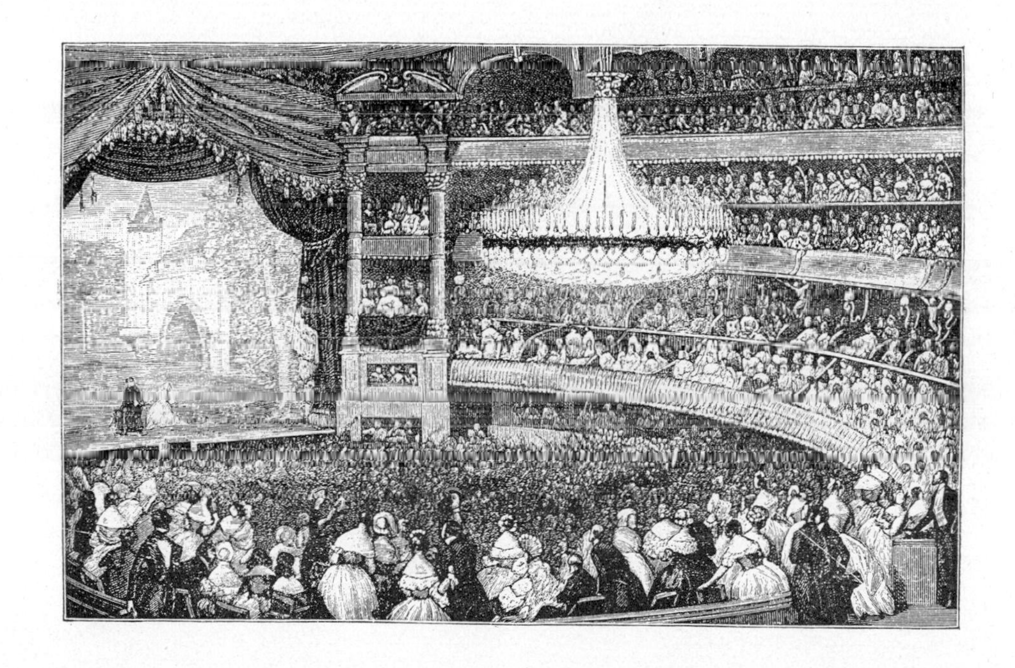

*Plate* 34 The "wing" setting grew out of the standardization of painted scenes. The stage picture was made up of a double row of parallel painted screens pushed in from the sides, before a painted backcloth. Even in interior scenes there were no side walls; only successive edges of the "flats" forming "wings" for entrance and exit. In this screen scene from *The School for Scandal* at the Drury Lane Theatre, London, the window and bookshelves are painted on the backdrop, and there are slid-in wings with painted architecture instead of walls with doors. The typical English forestage shown here, with portals, is almost the sole legacy from the Elizabethan playhouse; the rest all grew out of the introduction of the Italian style. The little scene from a German production of 1655, below, indicates how the edges of the wings caught the light and showed up as breaks in the picture, unless a very master of lighting was in charge.

*Plate* 35 Photographs of wing settings on a picture stage. The eighteenth-century Drottningholm Castle theatre in Sweden was recently restored after a long period of disuse, and these photographs were taken of the old-time settings still stored there. To the eyes of theatregoers of to-day, trained to realism, the painted wings and the sky "borders" of the street scene seem artificial enough; but it is possible to make out, if one looks close enough, that in the "cottage" setting considerable furniture is painted on the wings and backdrop, and that the latter bears a painted semblance of a raftered roof. Below is a drawing showing how the wings were constructed and attached to masts sliding in parallel grooves in the stage floor.

*Plate* 36 The half practicable, half-painted setting. An example of skilful coördination of built and painted-in-perspective scenery, as designed by Carl Friedrich Schinkel for *Kathchen von Heilbronn.* Typical nineteenth-century practice of the better sort. Below, a typical French example, by Rubé and Chaperon.

*Plate* 37 The effort to make the elaborate picture natural. Above, a decoration by Lavastre for *Tribut de Zamora*. Below, a setting for *Il Pirata*, an opera produced at Milan. On this page, a fire "effect" as seen from the auditorium and from back-stage.

*Plate* 38 By expending enough money to copy a great hall in every detail, the producer occasionally arrived at a true grandeur that would have satisfied even the later realists—but found then that his drama was burdened with insupportable waits for scene-changing. Two settings at the Italian Theatre in Paris.

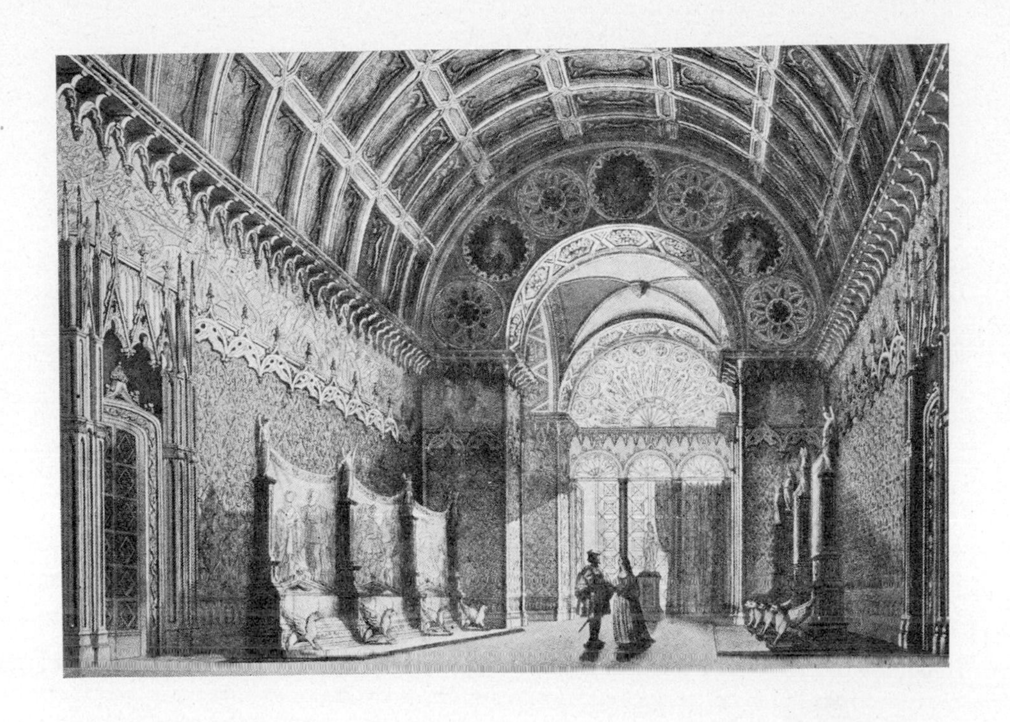

*Plate* 39 The romantic landscape painter triumphant. The forest of *Parsifal*, as seen in a production at Munich. Below is a "section" through the Paris Opera House, after a drawing by Karl Fichot and Henri Meyer, indicating the immensity of the late nineteenth-century stage in relation to the auditorium, and showing the method of hanging scenery, the maze of operating balconies and devices, and the several floors of machinery above and below the stage proper.

*Plate* 40 The typical late nineteenth-century painter's setting. Above, a scene from *Manon Lescaut* at the Metropolitan Opera House, New York. Below, a scene from *The Merchant of Venice* at the Comédie Française.

*Plate* 41 Naturalism triumphant, with painter's materials, in an exterior setting. Almost a perfect photograph of a place. Setting by Adolph Linnebach for *Wetterleuchten*, at the Dresden State Theatre.

*Plate* 42 Naturalism in interior scenes. Careful avoidance of the composed picture. An effort to make the stage room seem real by showing glimpses into other parts of the house. Settings for *The Cherry Orchard* and *The Three Sisters* at the Moscow Art Theatre.

*Plate* 43 Naturalism by multiplied casual detail. The realists lost the actor in a scene as distracting in its own natural way as the nineteenth-century painter's scene had been in its elaborate artificial way. Setting for *The Return of Peter Grimm* as produced by David Belasco.

# PART III

## ONE HUNDRED EXAMPLES OF MODERN STAGE DECORATION

*Plate* 44 *Setting by Lee Simonson* for Molnar's *Liliom* as produced by the New York Theatre Guild.

The current of twentieth-century decorative practice flows in two streams: the broader one in this sort of modified realistic picture setting; the narrower turning away from the depiction of actuality toward a stricter modernism based on a non-realistic, non-picturing stage without proscenium frame. This plate and those immediately following illustrate the best practice within the frame, the picture prettily simplified, made tasteful, composed. There is none of the old painted perspective here, no elaboration of detail, no scenic display; only a picture made largely with plastic materials, offering a fairly flat background for acting, lighted to be an aid to mood—even while remaining an illustration of some actual corner of nature somewhere.

*Plate* 45 *Setting by Rollo Peters* for Philip Moeller's *Mme. Sand.*

The same sort of tasteful simplification applied to an interior scene. It may be illuminating to compare this with plates 42 and 43.

*Plate* 46 *Design by Emil Orlik* for *The Winter's Tale:* "before the palace."

A sketch made for one of Max Reinhardt's early productions, 1906. The design was widely reproduced, and had influence on decorators in many countries. Below is added a thumbnail sketch by Ernst Stern for *Sumurun,* another Reinhardt production that influenced play-mounting outside Germany.

*Plate* 48 *Setting by Robert Edmond Jones* for Arthur Hopkins' production of *The Devil's Garden.*

In contrast to the preceding plate, a starkly simple scene, but composed with extraordinary fitness to the dramatic values involved. An accused postal clerk, in the isolated chair, is to be examined by inspectors grouped at the desk—in a room fairly breathing rigidity and lack of human sympathy.

*Plate* 49 *Setting by Cleon Throckmorton* for Eugene O'Neill's *The Moon of the Caribbees* as produced by the Provincetown Playhouse.

Not a thing that could be termed unrealistic; yet simplified, composed, and the central space kept free for acting—as contrasted with the elaborate ships that would have been built for this play twenty years earlier. Just as much of the ship as good dramatic sense and the tiny Provincetown stage would permit.

*Plate* 50 *Setting at the Moscow Art Theatre* for Andreieff's *Anathema*.

A similarly difficult problem, almost as simply solved. A little more reversion to "painty" methods, but with a flatness and a concentration achieved by the disposition of the main lines of the composition and the clever placing of the actors.

*Plate* 51 *Two settings by Woodman Thompson* for the Quinteros' *Malvaloca* as produced by the Actors' Theatre, New York.

The search for simplicity and economy led to the invention of "unit" settings, wherein certain portions of the first setting stand throughout all the scenes of the play. Here the arches are permanent, appearing with the slightest changes in both interior and exterior scenes.

*Plate* 52 *Two designs by Claude Bragdon* for Walter Hampden's production of *Hamlet*.

Here the units are movable, rearrangements of individual pieces affording new forms and differing atmosphere.

*Plate* 53 *Two settings by Boris Anisfeld* for the Chicago Opera Company's production of *The Love for Three Oranges.*

The entire forestage construction is permanent, with changing pictures beyond the archway. A half-formal, half-realistic method, with the unchanging formal elements affording a sense of unity and continuity.

*Plate* 54 *Design by Robert Edmond Jones* for *The Man Who Married a Dumb Wife,* as produced by Granville-Barker in New York.
Simplicity and stylization—and one of the earliest examples of "the new stagecraft" by an American designer, 1915.

*Plate* 55 *Design by Fritz Erler* for *Faust.*

One of the early examples of German simplification and stylization, for a production by Georg Fuchs at the Munich Art Theatre. This design received wide publicity throughout the theatre world, was published in Jacques Rouché's *l'Art Theatral Moderne* in Paris in 1910, and was copied into American publications among others. It was an early and successful demonstration of the values of "relief" staging, against a flat background, with a very few "plastic" units constituting all the "scenery." By way of contrast, here is a suggestion of the great spaces and elaborate building expended on the same scene by earlier designers, in a *décor* by the nineteenth-century designer Cambon.

*Plate* 56 *Design by Knut Strom and Rochus Gliese* for the sleep-walking scene of *Macbeth.*

Munich posteresque stylization at its best, in utterly simplified background, the one plastic construction conceived theatrically, the only notes of color supplied in the costumes. The picture stage stylized almost out of existence, to the point where it becomes formal stage.

*Plate* 57 *Setting by Joseph Urban* for *The Love of the Three Kings* at the Boston Opera.

Stylization according to a recognizable decorative mode. An illustration also of the use of a skeleton setting through many scenes, the portals at the front and the arch at the back being permanent.

*Plate* 58 *Setting by Raymond Jonson* for Cloyd Head's *Grotesques*, as produced by Maurice Browne at the Chicago Little Theatre.

The stylization found its origin in the author's conception of the play as "a decoration in black and white."

*Plate* 59 *Setting by James Reynolds* for *The Last Night of Don Juan,* as produced in New York by Macgowan, Jones and O'Neill.

Stylization out of a conception of Don Juan's Venice as lush, glamorous and decadently rococo.

*Plate* 60 *Setting by Norman Wilkinson* for Granville-Barker's production of *Twelfth Night.*

One of the earliest examples of stylization on the "regular" English stage, based on conventionalization in the German story-book manner.

*Plate* 61 *Sketches by Ernst Stern* of Reinhardt's revolving stage in process of being set with a composite scene, of which one view after another can be revealed to the audience by a slight turning of the central platform.

A description and floor-plans of scenes will be found on pages 56-58.

*Plate 62* *Two settings by Aline Bernstein* for productions at the Neighborhood Playhouse, New York: above, *The Little Clay Cart;* below, *The Dybbuk.*

Illustrating the use of plastic elements with a modified sky-dome for background, for two plays of very different scenic requirements.

*Plate 63* *Design by Leon Bakst* for *Sheherazade* as produced by Diaghilef's Russian Ballet in Paris. The old painter's method revived and pushed to the extreme of elaboration and colorfulness, to serve the sensuous dance-drama.

*Plate* 64 *Design by Leon Bakst,* typical of his largeness of conception and his method of deliberately dwarfing his dancers at certain times.

*Plate* 65 *Design by V. Egoroff* after the Moscow Art Theatre's production of Maeterlinck's *The Blue Bird*, as staged by Constantin Stanislavsky.

Poetic fairy-book stylization, quite in the sentimental-dream mood of the play.

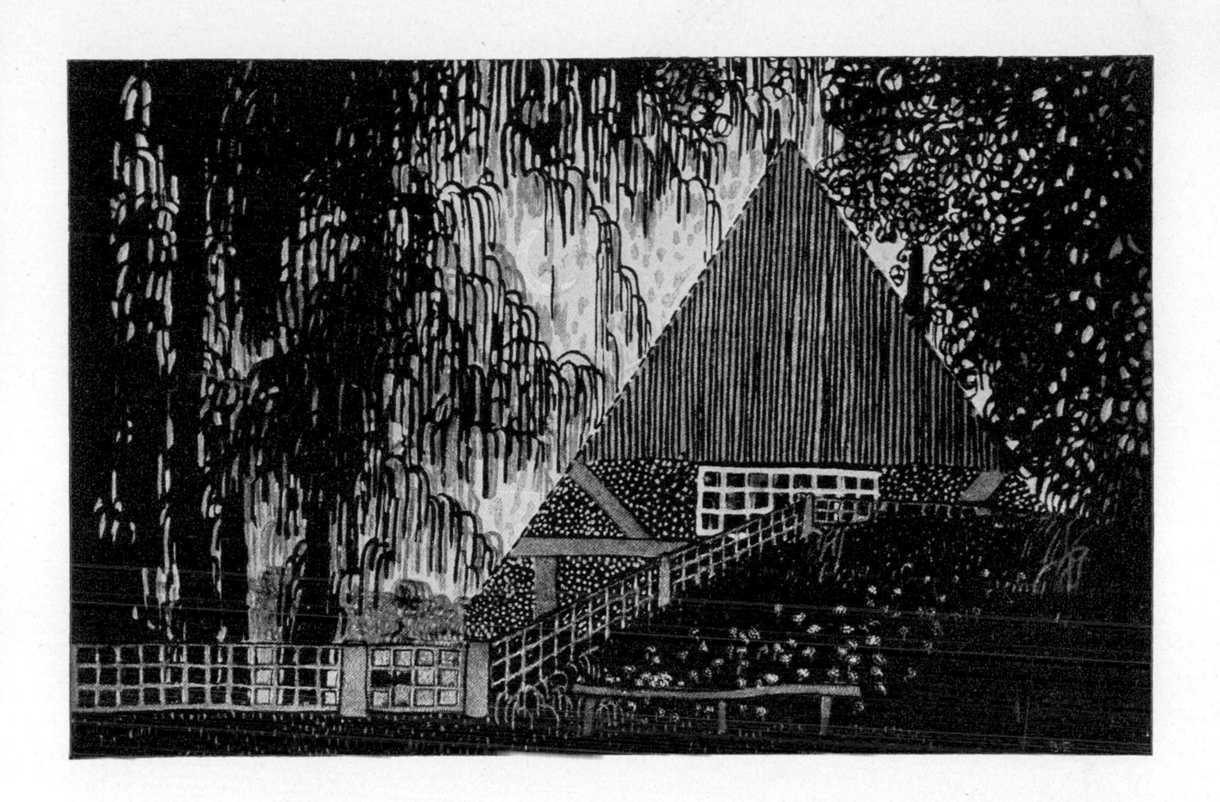

*Plate* 66 *Design by V. Egoroff* showing the "land of memory" scene in the Moscow Art Theatre production of *The Blue Bird*.

The picture conventionalized, made otherworldly, and wholly charming.

*Plate 67* *Design by Gordon Craig* for *Hamlet* . . . "I am thy father's spirit . . ."

Here the reader comes to the leader of the forces of revolt against realistic play-mounting. This is the turning point of this book between the two main divisions of twentieth-century staging: from now on there is evident a more or less complete abandonment of the realistic illusion, either by detailed depiction or by tasteful suggestion; the trend is all toward modern Expressionism, toward creation of a frankly theatric place for acting, toward abstraction, toward formal stages and space stages. Craig said, in briefest paraphrase: "Suppose we forget the picture, abandon depiction—why, we get back to *the theatre*."

*Plate* 68 *Design by Gordon Craig* for *Julius Caesar:* "Caesar's house."

*Plate* 69 *Design by Gordon Craig* for the sleep-walking scene in *Macbeth*.

*Plate 70* *Design by Gordon Craig* for *Macbeth:* "before the castle."

Here is the beginning of a great deal of later talk about noble simplicity and about plastic means.

*Plate 71* *A model by Gordon Craig* showing the use of his unit screen setting on a large stage.

*Plate* 72 *An etching by Gordon Craig* of a scene designed with screens.

*Plate* 73 *Two designs by Adolphe Appia* for *The Valkyrs.* Appia, fellow pioneer and prophet with Craig, likewise abandoned all but the last traces of the painter's method and the realist's conception. He simplified the scene for acting, and gained his "decorative" changes largely by means of light.

*Plate* 74 *The Rock of the Valkyrs* as designed by Appia. In 1899, when this notably sensitive rendering was first published, it was so revolutionary that few people would believe it was intended for a stage scene. For years Wagner's stage direction for this setting had been an invitation to scenic artists to spread themselves with acres of painted canvas and elaborate *papier-mâché* construction. Appia chose instead to think first of the actor in the scene.

*Plate* 75 *Design by Adolphe Appia* for *Parsifal:* the forest. 1899.

*Plate* 76 *Two scenes* from Max Reinhardt's production of *Hamlet*.

Illustrating how much the "practical" producers were influenced by the ideas of Craig and Appia, even so early as 1909.

*Plate 77* *Design by Robert Edmond Jones* for Sidney Howard's *Swords*, as produced in New York by Brock Pemberton.

*Plate 78* *Setting by Maxwell Armfield* for one of Ruth St. Denis' dance dramas.

When Craig and Appia challenged realism and undermined the painted-picture setting, every sort of flat unobtrusive background was tried out; and curtains dropped behind the actors were found to afford a particularly useful neutral setting. Often the fabric in folds was considered decorative enough. Here one sees curtains with the slightest suggestion of applied design.

*Plate* 79 *Scene from the Chicago Little Theatre Passion Play* as staged by Maurice Browne and Raymond Jonson.

The actors playing in silhouette against a curtain lighted from behind. Setting wholly lost in favor of light.

*Plate* 80 *Setting by Norman Wilkinson* for *A Midsummer Night's Dream,* as produced by Granville-Barker. One of the prettiest modes evolved along the way from realistic depiction toward formalization. The decorator applied his conventionalized design to the curtains, and then by hanging them in obvious folds forewarned his audience against seeking any sense of actuality in the scene.

*Plate* 81 *Design by Albert Rutherston* for *Cymbeline:* "before the cave of Belarius."

A curtain with conventionalized design made to serve even more particularized purposes, by grace of frank unreality.

*Plate* 82 *Two settings by Lee Simonson* for *As You Like It.* The curtain used with permanent portals to afford a formal stage, alternating with a revealed picture stage.

*Plate* 83 *Setting by Raymond Jonson* for *Medea*, as produced by the Chicago Little Theatre under the direction of Maurice Browne.

After curtains, screens took generous place on experimental stages in the march toward abstraction. Here the "decoration" is achieved largely in the marshaling of the actors and by lighting.

*Plate* 84 *Settings by Lee Simonson* for John Masefield's *The Faithful*, as produced by the New York Theatre Guild.

The breaking of the picture into the panels of the screen has the same effect as the curtain's folds in disarming the realism-seeking mind.

*Plate* 85 *Two designs by Hermann Rosse* for dance settings. Screens used decoratively but with the primary purpose of throwing the emphasis on the dancers. The one below was planned as an all-gold background.

*Plate* 86 *A screen designed by John Wenger.*

Intended to be an independent unit on a curtained stage, this screen with its decorative painting was designed largely as a formal element, a color spot in a larger abstract composition. Used with a few pieces of furniture it might merely dress an interior; alone on the stage it might become a desired suggestion of a garden or woods scene.

*Plate* 87 *Setting by Ljubo Babic* for *Twelfth Night*, as produced at the National Theatre in Prague.

A curtained stage with rounded screens used in various relationships as dictated by acting requirements.

*Plate* 88 *Setting by Sam Hume* for Lord Dunsany's *The Tents of the Arabs*, as produced at the Arts and Crafts Playhouse, Detroit.

One arrangement of an "adaptable" setting modeled after Craig's interchangeable screen scene.

*Plate* 89 *Design by Paul Nash* for *A Midsummer Night's Dream:* "the palace of Theseus."
Architectural, but with chief reliance upon abstract rather than stylistic elements.

*Plate* 90 *Design by Mordecai Gorelik* for *R.U.R.:* a laboratory.

Architecture carried beyond time and place by abstraction.

*Plate* 91 *Two settings utilizing geometric design.* Above, a setting by Robert R. Sharpe for *The Makropoulos Secret,* as produced at the Pasadena Community Playhouse. Below, a design by Enrico Prampolini, for a "plastic" scene.

Here there is a reversion to two-dimensional design in an effort to bring the values of abstract Expressionistic painting to the stage.

*Plate* 92 *An Expressionistic moving-picture setting.*
A group of German designers succeeded in applying the principles (and tricks) of Expressionist painting appropriately to scene-making, for the film *The Cabinet of Dr. Caligari*—a mode widely imitated on experimental stages, but usually resulting in obvious failure to make the painted trickery seem essentially theatrical.

*Plate* 93 *Design by Boris Anisfeld* for a dance-drama: *Preludes.*

The naïve decorative mode in modernist painting has seemed the only one successfully brought to the stage, and then only for a very special type of sensuous-dramatic production. In that field it has proved itself both adequate and charming.

*Plate* 94 *Design by M. Doboujinski* for *le Regiment qui Passe*, a divertissement of the *Chauve-Souris* Theatre of Nikita Balieff.

Naïve painting with a humorous note, in the spirit of the pretty fooling of Balieff's troupe.

ROGEL

*Plate* 95 *Design by Natalia Gontcharova* for *Coq d'Or*. The naïve-primitive mode, with a distinct "peasant art" flavor.

*Plate* 96 *Two revivals of the simultaneous scene*. Above, a design by Hermann Rosse for the New York production of *Mandragola;* below, a design by Otto Reigbert for an Expressionistic play by Georg Kaiser.

*Plate* 97 *Drawing by Louis Jouvet* of the architectural stage of the *Théâtre du Vieux Colombier*, the playhouse of Jacques Copeau in Paris. A permanent stage with a few movable units at the back. A naked stage that has proved more convincingly than any other the practicability of non-realistic, almost changeless play-mounting. Below is an outline sketch of Copeau's similar stage which he used briefly at the Garrick Theatre in New York.

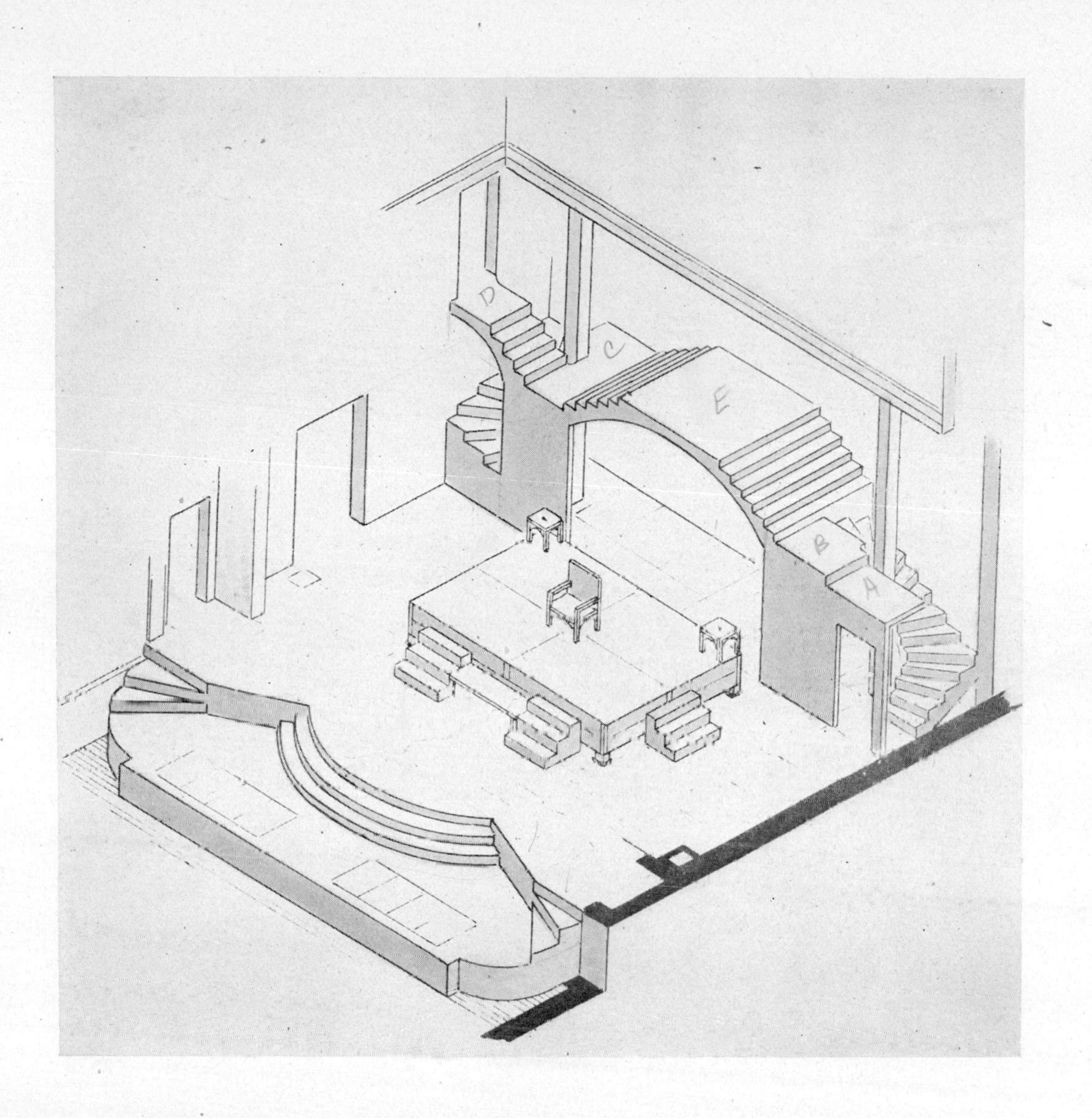
D
C
E
B
A

Plate 98 *Settings by Jacques Copeau and Louis Jouvet* for *The Brothers Karamazov* and for *La Carrosse du Saint-Sacrement* as arranged on the stage of the Vieux Colombier. From drawings by Robert Edmond Jones.

The permanent stage architecture is nine-tenths of any "decoration" in this theatre. Below is an outline cut after a model by Ladislas Medgyes for a formal stage.

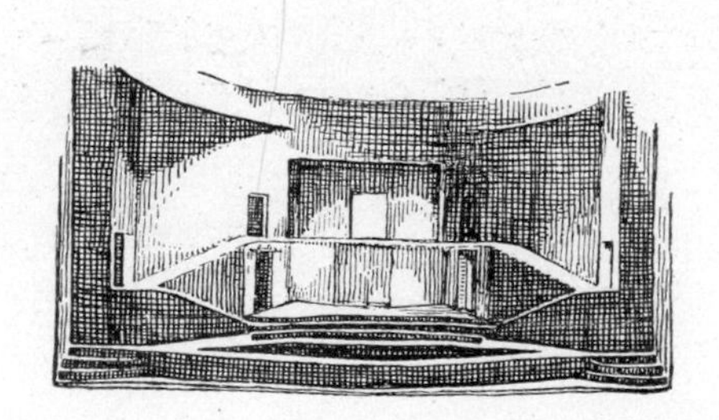

*Plate* 99 *The stage of the Marais Theatre* in Brussels, as designed under the direction of René Moulaert, with the guiding hand of Louis Jouvet.

A formal stage planned on the principle of one scene standing for all scenes, with only the slightest material changes—and flexible lighting—to accomplish differences of mood and suggestion. Below is a design by Alexander Bakshy for a formal stage.

*Plate* 100 *Three drawings by Andrew Stephenson of the Maddermarket Theatre stage* of the Norwich Players, Norwich, England.

Taking the historic Elizabethan playhouse as model, this group of amateur actors remodeled an old building into a theatre with a formal stage wherein certain architectural elements remain fixed and undisguised through a wide range of productions. Opposite, the stage is shown as it exists architecturally, and (below) as set with very simple additions for a scene in *Romeo and Juliet*. On this page is a drawing of the stage with panels set in to contract the playing space, and with changes in the inner stage, for a Restoration play. (The *Romeo and Juliet* scenes were designed by Andrew Stephenson; that for the Restoration play by O. P. Smyth.)

*Plate* 101 *Models by Norman-Bel Geddes* of stages for *The Mother of Christ* and *Lazarus Laughed.*

While the formal architectural stage is as much revival from the noblest theatres of the past as "modernist" invention, this type of sculptural stage is characteristically of the present and the future, a conception of the modern designer-director seeking more theatrical means for setting out the action, and made possible by the advance in lighting control. Under general lighting it is, not literally but atmospherically, one thing, and under localized lighting it may change to a score of different things.

*Plate* 102 *A model by Norman-Bel Geddes* of a stage for *King Lear*.
Below is a sketch after a model by Eduard Sturm for *Manfred*.

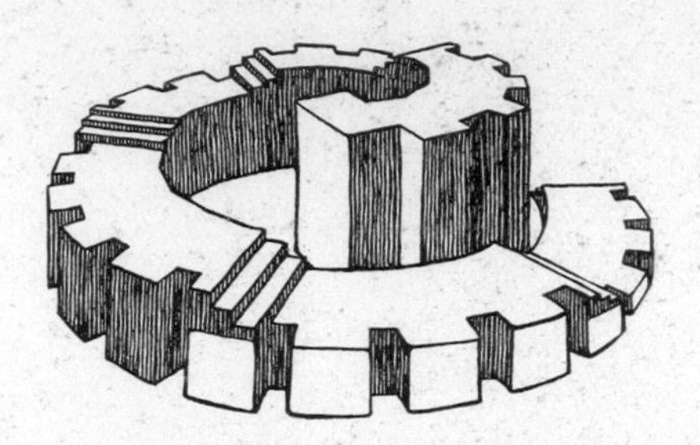

*Plate* 103 *Two views of the model by Norman-Bel Geddes* of a stage for *Dante*.

A very special stage designed for a wide range of "decoration" through lighting and the marshaling of actors.

*Plate* 104 *Designs by Donald Mitchell Oenslager* for scenes in *Das Rheingold* and *Götterdämmerung*, on a permanent stage projected for Wagner's *Ring*.

A stage construction based vaguely on the idea of the Tree of Existence, planned for acting the many scenes of the several operas without other changes than those accomplished by light.

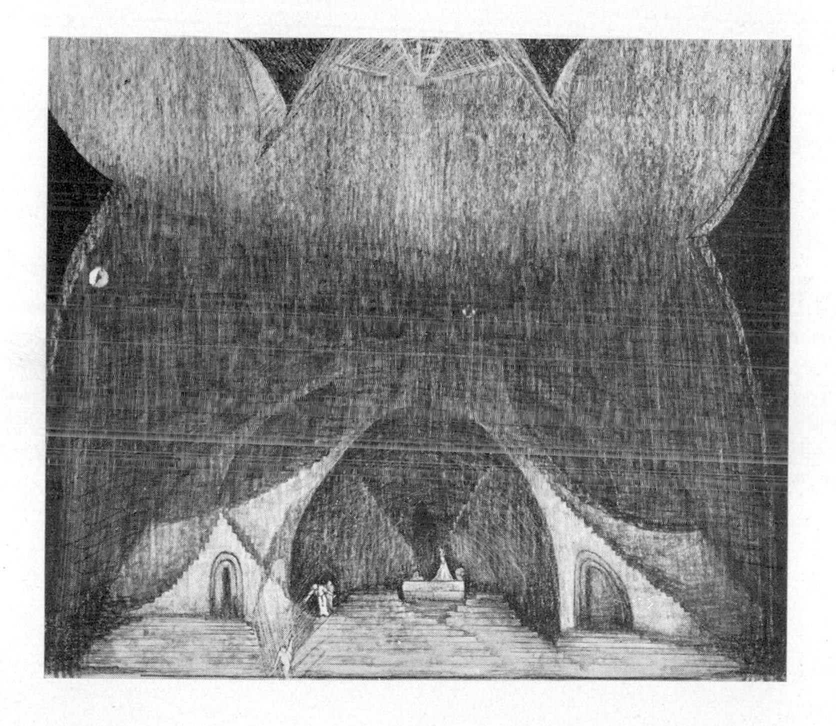

*Plate* 105 *A model by Jo Mielziner* for a presentation of *Faust*.

Planned for a revolving stage, this sculptural setting, in presenting a different angle to view and under different lighting, is designed to provide every scene necessary for the playing of *Faust*.

*Plate* 106 *Setting by T. C. Pillartz* for *Oedipus.*
Where the abstract screen setting and the sculptured stage meet.

*Plate* 107 *The formal stage* in the *Redoutensaal*, a palace ballroom in Vienna as remodeled into a theatre by Alfred Roller under the direction of Max Reinhardt. From a drawing by Robert Edmond Jones.

The architectural stage stylized from the existing decoration of the room.

*Plate* 108 *The tripartite stage* of the Decorative Arts Exposition Theatre at Paris, 1925, designed by A. and G. Perret and A. Granet.

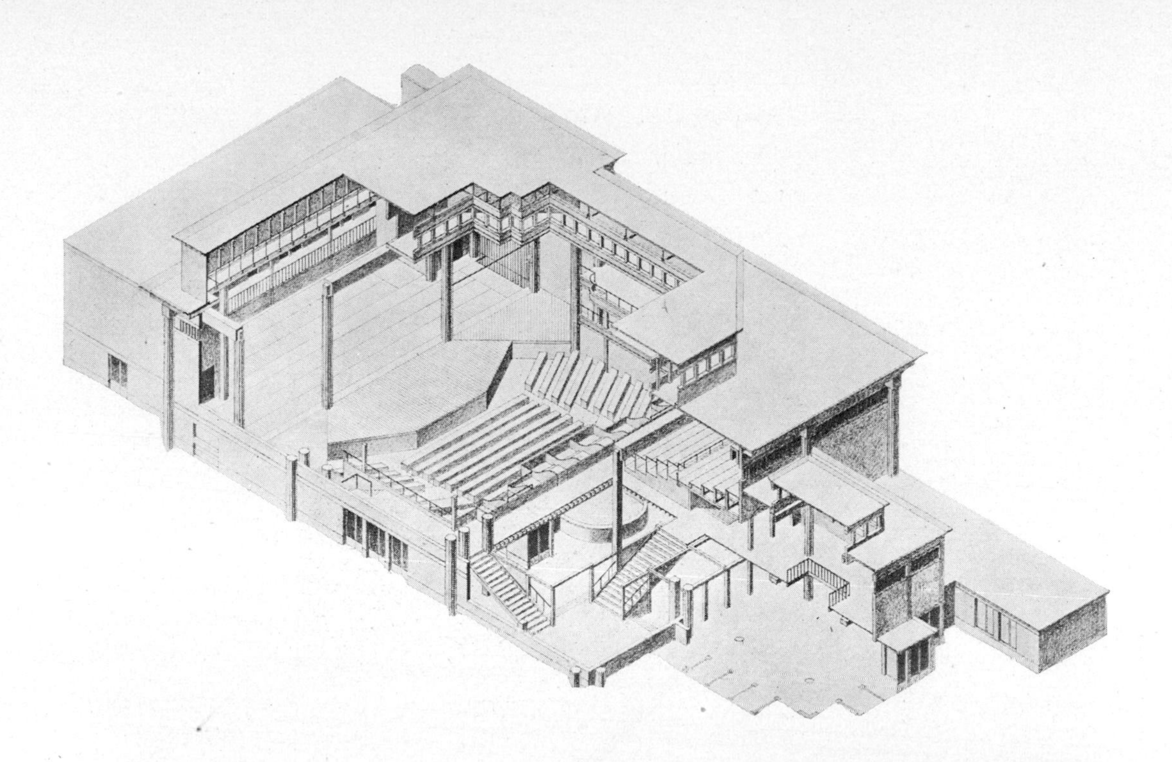

*Plate* 109 *Setting by Emil Pirchan* for *Othello*, as produced under the direction of Leopold Jessner at the State Theatre, Berlin. From a drawing by Robert Edmond Jones.

A shaped platform in space, with the barest anchor in reality; levels to afford variety of movement in the acting, and skilful lighting.

*Plate* 110 *Design by Ludwig Zuckermandel* for *Coriolanus*. If one elects to hold to the actuality of place, a suggestion of this sort set out in apparently boundless space is both dramatic and practicable—perhaps not on the average restricted American stage, but on the larger German ones with horizon-domes and flexible lighting equipment.

*Plate* 111 *Setting by Adolphe Appia* for Claudel's *The Tidings Brought to Mary.* 1914.

*Plate* 112 *Design by Adolphe Appia* for *Echo and Narcissus*. A stage designed for the Dalcroze Institute Theatre, 1920.

*Plate* 113 *Design by Adolphe Appia* for *Hamlet* . . . "The rest is silence."

Living space, living light, a very few simple architectural elements—these now seem to Appia best to set the actor out.

*Plate* 114 *Setting* for *Phedre,* as produced by Alexander Tairoff at the Kamerny Theatre, Moscow.
Composition in tilted planes and upright masses for dramatic effect. The two pictures show halves of the same setting, but in different scenes.

*Plate* 115 *Two settings by Lee Simonson* for *The Failures*, as produced by the New York Theatre Guild. Fragmentary bits of reality isolated on the space stage.

*Plate* 116 *Design by Robert Edmond Jones* for *Macbeth*, as produced by Arthur Hopkins in New York, 1921. Expressionistic use of vaguely suggestive elements on a space stage.

*Plate* 117 *Design by Robert Edmond Jones* for Maeterlinck's *The Seven Princesses.* Abstract setting designed for a space stage, and a forerunner of Constructivism. 1919.

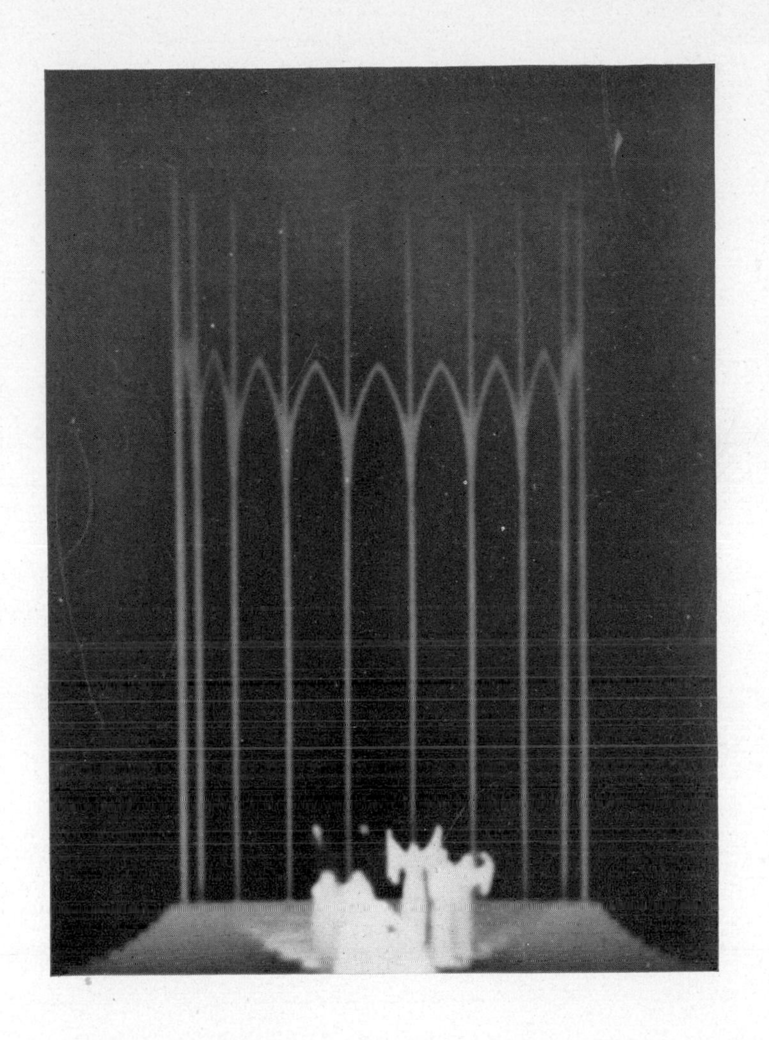

*Plate* 118 *Constructivist setting* by L. Popova for *le Cocu Magnifique*, as produced at Meyerhold's Theatre in Moscow. 1922.

The typical Constructivist arrangement of the "practicables" required by the action, with "decoration" rigidly suppressed. The original Constructivists avowed themselves anti-decorative; but they have achieved a decorativeness of their own sort, without reference to "styles," without ornament, and growing directly out of structure.

CR

*Plate* 119 *Setting by Isaac Rabinowitch* for *Lysistrata*, as produced by the Moscow Art Theatre Musical Studio.

Constructivism without the anti-decorative emphasis: the skeleton shaped with decorative intent, but on a typical curtainless stage, with all the scenes built into one scene. In this case the setting turned to give different faces to the audience.

*Plate* 120 *A Constructivist setting* for Wedekind's *Franziska* at the Raimund Theatre, Vienna; and a setting by J. Hofman for K. H. Hilar's production of *Hamlet* at the Prague National Theatre.

A typical "anti-decorative" Constructivist design contrasted with a carefully decorative bit set out on a "space stage."

IRQUE BUFFALO
Williams

*Plate* 122 *Designs by Louis Jouvet* for *Knock*.
The setting as background, but conceived non-pictorially, as an arrangement to show up the actors on a platform. The artist in this case disavows designing decorations: he merely diagrams a space for playing.

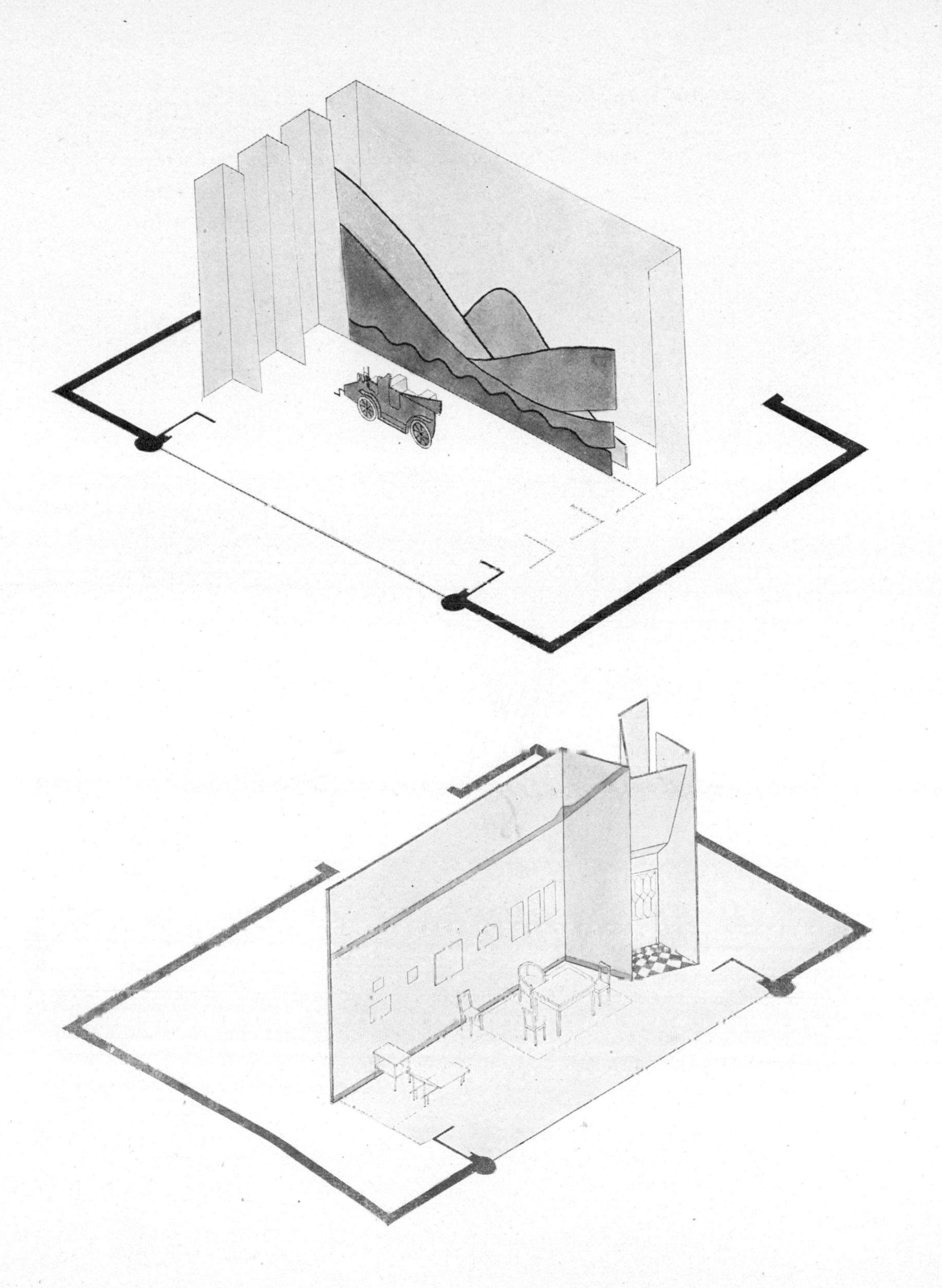

*Plate* 123 *Two settings by T. C. Pillartz,* for *Louis Ferdinand,* above, and *Sirocco,* below.

An appealing compromise between skeleton setting and highly selective realism. Distinctly the sense of a space stage, but with actual places unmistakably denoted in a few suggestive elements.

*Plate* 124 *Setting by Norman Edwards* for *The Marriage of Figaro* at the Eastman Theatre, Rochester; and a platform stage with screens used by Max Reinhardt at Salzburg.

*Plate* 125 *Two settings by Emil Pirchan* for Wedekind's *Marquis von Keith,* as produced under the direction of Leopold Jessner at the State Theatre, Berlin.

The interior scene grown very abstract, ceilingless, geometrical.

*Plate* 126 *Design by Robert Edmond Jones* for *The Buccaneer*, as produced in New York by Arthur Hopkins.

A stylized picture setting so carefully based on the acting values and so economical of detail that it approached the status of a formal stage.

# PART IV

## INDEX

# INDEX

# INDEX

# INDEX

# INDEX

# INDEX

# INDEX

# INDEX

# INDEX

# INDEX